Helion & Company Limited
Unit 8 Amherst Business Centre
Budbrooke Road
Warwick
CV34 5WE
England
Tel. 01926 499 619
Email: info@helion.co.uk
Website: www.helion.co.uk
Twitter: @helionbooks
https://helionbooks.wordpress.com/

Designed and typeset by Mach 3 Solutions (www.mach3solutions.co.uk)
Cover design by Paul Hewitt, Battlefield Design (www.battlefield-design.co.uk)

Front cover illustration: During a free-hunting mission on 13 July 1937, over the Badajoz road between Madrid and Navalcarnero, a FARE patrol made up of three Polikarpov I-16s flown by the Americans Frank Tinker and Albert John Baumler and the Soviet Erlykin spotted a group of Italian bombers returning from a mission against Madrid. During the pursuit, two Messerschmitt Bf 109B-1s of the Condor Legion appeared from above, firing at long range. Baumler and Erlykin engaged one of them while Tinker (with five victories in Spain) took on the other, piloted by Guido Höness (already credited with three victories in Spain). Höness accepted combat with Tinker's aircraft, but after executing a spiral Tinker managed to turn the engagement to his advantage. On the third burst he fired—by then almost at point-blank range—Tinker struck the German aircraft, whose engine began to smoke and immediately burst into flames that enveloped the cockpit, causing the German pilot to crash to the east of Navalcarnero. This shoot-down was the first suffered by a Messerschmitt Bf 109 in Spanish skies. (Artwork by Elena Stanilevich © Helion & Company 2025)

ISBN 978-1-804517-19-2

British Library Cataloguing-in-Publication Data
A catalogue record for this book is available from the British Library

Contents

Note: In order to simplify the use of this book, all names, locations and geographic designations are as provided in *The Times World Atlas*, or other traditionally accepted major sources of reference, as of the time of described events.

ACKNOWLEDGEMENTS AND DEDICATIONS

In Memoriam
Eduardo Gil Barba
Juan Arráez Cerdá

Dedication
To Solete, my life.
To my parents, Salud and Eduardo.
To Caco, Iñigo, Ibón and June.
To Merce.
To my grandparents Mercedes, Salud, Mami, Manuel and Juan.
To Ángel el "Garcí".
To Juan Arráez.

Acknowledgements to:
Marisol García Gómez, Ricardo Ramallo Gil, Francisco Javier Santiago Elviro.

ABBREVIATIONS AND ACRONYMS

AL	*Aviazione Legionaria* (Legionary Aviation)
AN	*Aviación Nacional* (National Aviation)
FARE	*Fuerzas Aéreas de la República Española* (Air Forces of the Spanish Republic)
LAPE	*Líneas Aero-Postales Españolas* (Spanish Post Air Lines)
SCW	Spanish Civil War
SEPEWE	*Syndykat Eksportu Przemysłu Wojennego* (War Industries Export Syndicate)

PREFACE

Dear reader, in this first volume you will learn in great detail about the main actions of the Spanish Civil War during its first two years: 1936 and 1937. We will be able to appreciate throughout the book the almost immediate evolution of an antiquated pre-SCW Spanish air force to become the air forces of both sides, possibly the most modern in Europe. This was due to the arrival of large numbers of aircraft and flight personnel (pilots, mechanics, etc.) from the leading countries in the mid-1930s in Europe and the world: we are referring to Germany, Italy and the Soviet Union. Although it is true that aircraft from other countries also arrived in Spain, such as France or the United States, they were not as decisive in the fighting as those from the aforementioned countries.

The German *Luftwaffe* appeared in Spain in the form of the so-called Condor Legion, which achieved worldwide fame and enabled it to begin to train pilots who would become great aces in the Second World War. Similarly, the Italian *Regia Aeronautica* flew over Spain with the Aviation of the Tercio and later with the *Aviazione Legionaria*. In the case of the Soviet Union, although Soviet aircraft were flown by Soviet pilots, they never became an official unit of the Soviet Air Force or VVS (*Voyenno-vozdushnye sily*).

In this book we can also relive the evolution in air combat tactics, both in fighters and bombers or attack aircraft, largely due to the presence in Spain of faster aircraft, with more weapons and greater flight range. Aviation, which was initially just another point of support for the ground troops, would become decisive for the final outcome of the battle.

From the end of 1936 onwards, the skies over Spain became a great training ground for German, Italian and Soviet pilots to test their most modern aircraft in order to draw conclusions about how to use them. The turbulent Europe of the second half of the 1930s saw the possibility of war fast approaching and everyone wanted to be prepared for it in case it started, as it sadly did in September 1939.

Volume 1 of the book will be followed with Volume 2, in which we will narrate the decisive moments that led to the final victory of the rebel troops under the command of Francisco Franco, in which aviation played a decisive role.

1

BEFORE THE WAR

Political Context in Spain up to 1936

After the elections held on 12 April 1931 and the Republican-Socialist victory, King Alfonso XIII decided to go into exile on Tuesday 14 April in view of the possibility of clashes between the army and the *Guardia Civil* (Civil Guards) and the thousands of pro-Republic demonstrators flooding the country. Immediately in Madrid, the Republican-Socialist Committee established the 2nd Spanish Republic in Spain, presided over by Niceto Alcalá Zamora, with Manuel Azaña as Prime Minister. The 2nd Republic had detractors on one side, in the form of monarchists, the African military, the Church, and big businessmen, and on the other anarchists such as the CNT and the FAI, which led to great political instability that culminated in a failed coup d'état led by General Sanjurjo in August 1932.

In September 1933 the political coalition headed by Manuel Azaña broke up and elections were called for November 1933. The CEDA (*Confederación Española de Derechas Autónomas*) and the Republican Centre-Right of the *Partido Republicano Radical* (Radical Republican Party) were the victors. But the mood in Spain was not calm and in October 1934 a socialist insurrection against the government failed. These events led the CEDA to consider it necessary to win the presidency of the government in order to bring about a radical change in the country's government.

Three Nieuport 52C.1s manufactured in Spain by La Hispano-Suiza fly over Getafe airfield (Madrid) where one of the two Cierva C.30A two-seater gyroplanes was stationed.

A Savoia S.62 at San Javier (Murcia). This seaplane of Italian origin was manufactured under licence in Spain from 1931 to 1936 (40 plus one aircraft imported from Italy). At the beginning of the war, five based in Marín (Pontevedra) remained in rebel hands and 30 in government hands.

Despite this, the president of the Republic, Alcalá Zamora, refused to give power to the CEDA – which had not proclaimed its loyalty to the Republic – and commissioned the formation of an independent centre-Right government. This government remained in power until new elections were called for 16 February 1936. The results of these elections showed how divided the Spanish population was, with 47.1 percent of the votes going to the Left wing and 45.6 percent to the Right wing. Despite this equality, on Wednesday 19 February 1936, Manuel Azaña formed a new government consisting only of Left-wing Republican ministers, leaving the Right out of power. Not content with that, he tried to remove the military commanders of known anti-republicanism from positions of power. On 10 May 1936, Manuel Azaña took over as president of the Spanish Republic and the outlook was not promising, as the discontent on the Right was compounded by protests and strikes on the Left. In this hostile climate the Spanish Falange (a fascist political party) and various Left-wing workers' organisations provoked numerous violent acts throughout the country. Discontent was evident in large parts of the population, with clashes between military and Rightists against storm troopers and Leftists not uncommon.

The *pistolerism* practised in those months by individuals of both the extreme Right and the extreme Left claimed the life of Lieutenant Castillo, a member of the Assault Guards, on 12 July. Following the spiral of violent deaths in revenge for the previous ones, the next day some Assault Guards took Calvo Sotelo, head of the Nationalist Bloc (he can also be called a National, although in this text we have chosen to use this terminology), from his home, which was the trigger for the events that were to follow.

Meanwhile, the feeling of the country's collapse grew among a group of military officers led by General Emilio Mola, who from the end of April took the lead in a coup plot aimed at creating a military junta, headed by General Sanjurjo, to govern the country.

The possibility of a return was so real that on 16 July the government ordered the destroyer *Churruca* to leave for Algeciras and the gunboat *Dato* to anchor in Ceuta, all in anticipation of a possible transport of troops from Africa to the mainland. That same night Franco embarked in Tenerife and headed for Las Palmas, where a De Havilland Dragon Rapide rented from the British Olley Airways Company was waiting to take him to Spanish Morocco to take command of the African army. The main thrust of the coup d'état that was being prepared was to be carried out by the Spanish military forces deployed in North Africa. The military uprising began in Melilla on 17 July 1936 and soon spread to the Iberian Peninsula. Contrary to expectations, government resistance meant that the coup d'état was unsuccessful and the whole thing dragged on until it became a veritable civil war.

Several Nieuport 52C.1s belonging to Group 11 stationed at Getafe airfield before the start of the SCW.

A magnificent photograph taken in 1935 of a Nieuport 52C.1 belonging to *Grupo 11* (Group 11) based at Getafe. This Group had two squadrons characterised by their black panther emblem. The aircraft carries the tricolour flag of the Republic of Spain, as well as cockades on and under the wings with the tricolour cockade (red-yellow-purple).

Aeronautics in July 1936

In July 1936, the body that governed aerial activity in Spain was the General Directorate of Aeronautics, to which Military Aviation, Naval Aviation, Civil Aeronautics and the National Meteorological Service reported directly to the Minister of War.

Table 1: Organisation of the Military Aviation in March 1936

Base	Units
Squadra Nº1	
Getafe	No. 11 Group with 2 Ni52C.1 Fighter Squadrons
	No. 31 Group with 2 Reconnaissance Squadrons (Br. XIX), with 1 patrol deployed in the Sahara
	No. 21 Group with 3 Reconnaissance Squadrons (Br. XIX)
Squadra Nº2	
Seville	No. 22 Group with 2 Reconnaissance Squadrons (Br. XIX)
	1 Fighter Squadron with Ni52C.1
Squadra Nº3	
Logroño	No. 23 Group with 3 Reconnaissance Squadrons (Br. XIX)
Barcelona	No. 13 Group with 2 Ni52C.1 Fighter Squadrons
African Air Force	
Melilla	Seaplane Squadron (Dornier Wal)
	2 Patrols of the 2nd Reconnaissance Squadron (Br. XIX)
Tetuán	1st Reconnaissance Squadron (Br. XIX)
Larache	1 Patrol of the 2nd Reconnaissance Squadron (Br. XIX)
Sahara	1 Fokker F.VII Squadron
Instructional Units	
Los Alcázares	Firing and bombing school: Y-2 Squadron (Br. XIX), No. 6 Group with 2 Squadrons (Dornier Wal) with a patrol deployed in Mallorca
Alcalá de Henares	Flying and Combat School: 2 Patrols (DH.89 and Fokker F.VII)
Four Winds	Observer School: Y-1 Squadron (Br. XIX)

Table 2: Pre-SCW Naval Aviation organisation, 1936

Base	Units
San Javier	Torpederos Squadrilla, equipped with CASA-Vickers Vildebeest
	Reconnaissance Squadrilla, equipped with Savoia-Marchetti S.62
	Bombing Squadrilla, equipped with Dornier Wal
	Training And Combat Squadrilla, equipped with Savoia-Marchetti S.62 seaplanes, Hispano E-30, CASA-III, Dornier Wal and C.30 gyroplanes

As shown in Tables 1 and 2, in 1936 Spanish aeronautics was at a critical moment. The materiel was becoming obsolete and in most cases it was necessary to renew the aircraft. The main fighter aircraft was the Nieuport-Delage Ni52C.1 built under licence by Hispano but there were already plans to replace it with a more modern model. The two competitors to be Spain's new fighter were the Hawker Fury and the Boeing P-26 (281). In fact, at the start of the SCW, there were three Hawker Furies in Spain – disassembled and destined for Hispano in Guadalajara where, under patent, it was planned to manufacture this model as the Hawker Hispano Fury – and one Boeing 281, which had also been tested. The four aircraft, after being armed, would form part of the FARE (*Fuerzas Aéreas de la República Española*, Air Forces of the Spanish Republic) at the beginning of the SCW.

As a reconnaissance and light bomber, the aviation branch used the Breguet XIX. Although it had a long history in the world of big raids, this aircraft was completely obsolete, but was nevertheless used as a reconnaissance and bombing aircraft (carrying up to 400kg of bombs). The Br. XIX was to be replaced by an as yet undetermined model, but the uprising and subsequent civil war prevented the plans from being carried out. Fokker F.VIIBs were used as bombers, some of which had been built under licence by Loring in Madrid. This aircraft was also used as a transport, and was widely used by both sides in the early days of the SCW. Spain also had a good number of seaplanes, which were very useful due to the country's long coastline. The Dornier Wal and the Savoia S.62 would play an important role on both sides

The Navy's aviation had Dornier Wal seaplanes and three squadrons of Vickers Vildebeest torpedo planes (25 land-based and two seaplanes). It also had some old Macchi seaplanes and Martinsyde landplanes.

Over the next few months, a number of changes took place which resulted in 241 operational aircraft (plus 72 second line) on 1 July 1936.

Nieuport 52C.1s belonging to *Grupo 13* based in Barcelona. The *Grupo 13* emblem, a four-leaf clover, is visible. The photograph was taken in 1935 at San Javier.

A frosty morning at El Prat airfield (Barcelona) where the Nieuport 52C.1s of *Grupo 13* were based.

The Hawker Fury (in its Spanish version called the Spanish Fury) was to have been the main fighter of the Republic. It was to replace the venerable Nieuport 52C.1 as the spearhead of Spanish aviation, but the onset of the SCW prevented these plans from coming to fruition.

Impressive photograph of several Nieuport 52C.1s of the *Grupo 12* in formation during a flight. At the start of the SCW, *Grupo 12* was disbanded.

One of the Hispano Nieuport 52C.1s of the pre-SCW *Grupo 11* as can be identified by its black panther emblem. Two more aircraft of the same type are seen in the background.

2

1936

The Uprising in Africa and the Conquest of Seville, 17 and 18 July

After the assassination of Calvo Sotelo on 13 July 1936 by Leftists of the state police, the imminence of armed confrontation in July 1936 was noticeable in the atmosphere amongst the military, and the undecided finally made up their minds. Franco and General Mola agreed on the uprising and the attempted coup d'état began.

By order of General Mola, the army in Africa was to be quartered from 17:00 on the 17th for action the following day. But the uprising was brought forward in Melilla by a leak that precipitated events.

As for Military Aviation, although the pilots were often obedient to their chiefs, other pilots expressed their disagreement by fleeing with their planes to their preferred side. In North Africa, the Sania Ramel airfield at Tetouan, and the Atalayón sea base at Melilla, although they remained loyal to the government, were occupied by army troops. For their part, those at Aumara (Larache) and Tauima (Melilla) joined the rebel forces. Cabo Juby accepted the government's order to transfer his three Fokker F.VII trimotors to Tablada (Seville) (the fourth was in Madrid), which would end up in the hands of the rebels.

A Nieuport 52C.1 at Tablada airfield (Seville), where the *Grupo 12* (Group 12), which had only one squadron before the war began, was based.

A Nieuport 52C.1 belonging to *Grupo 12* with the leaping deer emblem that remained in the hands of the Republicans at the start of the SCW.

A DH.83 Gox Moth belonging to the rebel side waits for the next flight.

At the start of the SCW, two of the Spanish-owned Dragon Rapides were left in the hands of the rebels, who made good use of them.

As mentioned above, two Fokker F.VIIs and a DC-2 of the Spanish airline *Líneas Aero-Postales Españolas* (LAPE, Spanish Post Air Lines) were assembled at Tablada airfield in Seville on the morning of the 18th with orders to bomb Morocco. The Fokker did so over the air bases, but the DC-2 was damaged on the ground by Captain Carlos Martínez Vara de Rey. At 15:00 a second DC-2 arrived from Madrid, which bombed Ceuta, Larache and Tetuán together with the two F.VIIs.

The LAPE planes returned to Barajas, except for the damaged DC-2, and two Fokker aircraft from Cabo Juby remained in Tablada, arriving mid-afternoon. The third, which followed them, would land in Larache. The important air base at Tablada seemed of great importance to the rebels as one of their objectives, so they sent an emissary to try to convince their commander-in-chief, Martínez. Although unsuccessful at first, after seeing how the government troops had been defeated in the city and the civilian government had fallen, he finally surrendered.

Above: The four Spanish DC-2s belonging to the LAPE (*Líneas Aéreas Postales Españolas*, Spanish Post Air Lines) at the start of the SCW, three were on the government side and one on the rebel side. These aircraft were used as transports and bombers.

Right: Close-up of several North African soldiers belonging to the rebel side next to the only DC-2 that fell into their hands. This aircraft was "baptised" with the name *Vara de Rey* after the soldier who captured it in Seville.

The Division of the Air Force

When the coup failed in Barcelona on 19 July and in Madrid on 20 July, the situation in Spain descended into civil war. The Republican government controlled a large part of Spain: the mining areas in the north, the Levant coast and the industrial areas of the Basque Country and Catalonia, while the rebels controlled Galicia, part of Castile, León, a large part of Aragón, the Spanish possessions in North Africa, as well as the cities of Córdoba, Seville, Granada and Cádiz.

The failure of the coup d'état as such divided Spain into two sides that prepared for war. Consequently, the Military Aviation was also divided. The government forces maintained control over some 200 aircraft while the rebels or Nationalists seized some 100. Despite the smaller numbers, the good use made of them by the rebels and the mismanagement of the Republic's aviation would balance the scales in the early stages.

It is quite possible that the SCW would have gone differently if the Republic had gained control of the skies over the Strait of Gibraltar and the northern part of the Moroccan protectorate. This was caused by an accumulation of circumstances, three of which stand out:

Firstly, before the uprising, the Republican side had accumulated the bulk of its aviation at the airfields near Madrid (Cuatro Vientos, Getafe, Barajas and Escuela de Caza de Alcalá de Henares) and Barcelona (Prat airfield and the Naval Aeronautics base). There were also some 100 aircraft left at the Los Alcázares base in Murcia, which, despite the proximity of Andalusia, were not transferred to that theatre of operations, which seemed decisive with the air bridge across the strait as will be seen later. Whether due to a lack of pilots (many had joined the rebel side) or for other reasons, the airlift took place with few incidents.

One of the Nieuport 52C.1s belonging to the only Squadron of *Grupo 12*. At the beginning of the SCW some 50 Nieuport 52C.1s were held by the Spanish government, while some 15 were held by the rebels.

Secondly, the aforementioned capture of the Tablada airfield in Seville, which allowed the Nationalists to have a large airfield in a city of great importance in the south of Spain and therefore a good destination for the troops coming from Africa.

Thirdly, the swift action of the Nationalist side to obtain aircraft from Germany and Italy (in particular the Ju 52 and SM.81 transports).

Several Breguet XIXs belonging to the Republicans ready for take-off on a new mission.

Some 80 Breguet XIXs remained in the hands of the Republicans (like the ones pictured here on the Central Operations Front) when the SCW started.

Several Republican Breguet XIXs belonging to the Night Flying School at their base at El Carmolí.

A Nieuport 52C.1 attached to Group 11 of the Nationalist side with its new insignia.

The only Hawker Fury (4W-1) belonging to the rebel side after being captured from the Republicans at Tablada airfield (Seville). This aircraft was assigned to Group 4, surviving the war (until 1950).

The approximate distribution after the first days of the SCW of the main aircraft was as shown in Table 3.

Table 3: Distribution of aircraft in the opening days of the Spanish Civil War

Plane	Government	Rebels
Ni52C.1	50	15
Br. XIX	80	70
Vickers Vildebeest	27	0
Fokker F.VIIb/3m	8	3
Dornier Wal	13	13
Savoia S.62	30	5
Macchi M.18	10	0
Hawker Fury	3	0
Boeing 281	1	0
Douglas DC-2	3	1

In the rebel zone, as they had not managed to take control of the whole country, their areas of influence meant that three aeronautical nuclei were isolated, depending on the generals who controlled the respective territories. Thus, we could speak of Mola's aviation (Northern Air Forces), Queipo de Llano's aviation (Southern Air Forces) and Franco's aviation (African Air Forces). In fact, at first, the only fighters available to the rebel side were those based in Seville, from the recently disbanded Seville Squadron and a damaged Ni52C.1 at the Granada airfield.

On 18 July, 10 Dornier Wal were at the bases of El Atalayón (Melilla) and Pollensa (Mallorca) but with damaged engines. These aircraft were put into service at the beginning of August after the arrival of 20 new Isotta-Fraschini Asso 500 engines from Italy. With these aircraft in service, the 1-G-70 Group was created, made up of the 1-E-70 and 2-E-70 squadrons.

Other seaplanes that remained in the hands of the rebels were five S.62s that were deployed in Marín (Pontevedra), three of which were sent to the strait sector, but one was destroyed on arrival in Ceuta and the other two were not in adequate operational condition.

A Fokker F.VII 3m belonging to the rebel side. These aircraft proved very useful during the airlift in the Strait of Gibraltar between July and November 1936.

One of the Fokker F.VII 3m belonging to the National Aviation during a flight. This model of aircraft managed to transport eight battalions of indigenous infantry troops from North Africa to the Iberian Peninsula between 20 July and 4 August 1936.

The Fokker F.VII *Veterano* (Veteran) along with *Abuelo* (Grandfather) and *Viejo* (Old Man) were the three aircraft of this model that formed part of the rebel side. They were used for the air bridge between Africa and the Iberian Peninsula, as well as to harass the Republican fleet or on different combat fronts.

The Air Bridge Between North Africa and the Iberian Peninsula

One of the key factors in the beginning of the SCW was the transfer of Spanish troops from North Africa to the Iberian Peninsula. This could not be done by sea as it was dominated by the Republican fleet, so it was decided to initiate what was to be the first air bridge in history. At first it was carried out with only the aircraft available, but was later supported by modern Italian and German aircraft.

The Republican fleet had at least 50 warships, including a battleship, *Jaime I*, three cruisers, two flotillas of destroyers and two flotillas of submarines. Against them, the rebel side had the gunboat *Dato*, the torpedo boat 19 and some coastguard ships that were incapable of facing the Republicans on equal terms.

Having lost the possibility of the African Army's passage by boat, a meeting of senior commanders was convened in Tetuán, attended by Kindelán, who decided to use the only route that remained open: the air. Of the 23 land-based multi-engined aircraft that the rebels had (10 military ones; five F.VIIs, four DC-2s and a Ford from LAPE; and three with lesser transport possibilities), Kindelán only had five, one in the North and four at his disposal (three Fokker F.VIIs from the 20th and a DC-2 from the 25th of July). With these, the daytime transport of the army began from Tetuán to Seville (later to Jerez), alternating with reconnaissance and night bombing raids to points as far away as Albacete and Madrid. The initial airlift was from Tetuán to Seville, although later importance was also given to the shorter, and therefore faster and less fuel-consuming, Ceuta to Algeciras airlift.

The airlift began on 20 July 1936 using three Fokker F.VII 3m as the main means. These were the Fokker that was diverted by Captain Ureña to Larache (which took a lieutenant and nine legionnaires to Seville to begin the airlift) and the two captured at Tablada. In addition, other aircraft of very different types took part in this operation. In fact, at the start of the operation, any aircraft of any capacity could be used to transport troops. Thus, there are the cases of the Savoia S.62 (with four soldiers in each plane per trip to Algeciras) or also seaplanes such as the Dornier Wal (piloted by Lieutenant Ruiz de la Puente de la Aeronáutica Naval) which made the Ceuta–Algeciras crossing multiple times carrying 11 and up to 13 legionnaires or *regulares* on each flight.

The airlift was also joined by the DC-2 damaged by Vara de Rey in Tablada and quickly repaired to be manned by Carlos Haya. The arrival of these troops in Cádiz and Seville allowed the rebels to establish their control over these territories and begin their advance both to the north and to the east. The setting up of an intermediate airfield at Jerez would allow the planes to take less time on their missions with less fuel consumption than if they had to fly a few kilometres further north towards Seville.

With so few men, six battalions (4th, 5th and 6th *Banderas* of the Tercio, 1st and 2nd *Tabores* of the *Grupo de Regulares de Tetuán* and 3rd of the *Grupo de Larache*) went to the Iberian Peninsula until 7 August.

A Dornier Wal seaplane at anchor next to a Pro-Revolutionary warship.

Another very important element in this operation was the arrival of the first German-supplied Ju 52, which had belonged to *Lufthansa*. As early as August, 10 Junkers Ju 52s joined them, increasing the number of men transported to the Peninsula, although they were dedicated exclusively to the airlift. In seven days, from 8 to 14 August, four more battalions were transported to the Iberian Peninsula (2nd Bandera of the Tercio, two tabores from Al Hoceima and one from Larache).

Despite the strategic importance of this operation, the Republic did not make a great effort to prevent the air crossing of the Strait of Gibraltar by troops in slow, poorly armed transport planes that would have been easily shot down by Ni52 fighters. The only protection the airlift planes initially had were three Ni52s that had been captured in Seville. So, from Los Alcázares, their only major military airfield close to the operation, their aircraft were more dedicated to protecting Cartagena and attacking Granada rather than looking towards the Strait of Gibraltar.

Instead, Republican aviation was concentrated in the Madrid area, as well as in Los Alcáceres, and the fighting was reduced to the battle between the Dornier Wal and Savoia S.62 seaplanes. In these few aerial clashes, the auxiliary Celestino Ramos and Naval Lieutenant Boada, of the Naval Air Force, with the complement of Lieutenant Pando and the mechanic Navarro flying a Dornier Wal 2 shot down a Republican Savoia S.62 from Santiago de la Ribera that was going to bombard Algeciras, being in turn shot down by the submarine C-4. Navy lieutenants Ruiz de la Puente and Rodolfo Bay sank the submarine B-5.

Two field batteries were also transported by air, but the heavy weapons and vehicles required a ship to transport them. At least one convoy was needed to carry out the mission but the Republican fleet was unwilling to relinquish control of the Strait of Gibraltar. It was only when the Savoia SM.81s arrived (when petrol with the right octane rating became available) that a sea convoy was put in place to leave on 5 August 1936. One of the Nationalist Dornier Wals discovered the Republican destroyer *Lepanto* at dawn (07:00) on a patrol flight and bombed it from 300 metres, causing several casualties and forcing it to take shelter in Gibraltar. The seaplane was supported by a patrol of Ju 52s and an SM.81 which bombed the destroyer in Gibraltar's territory.

At seven o'clock in the evening, an hour after the departure of the convoy which had been delayed by the presence of the *Lepanto* in Gibraltar, the destroyer *Alcalá Galiano* was discovered with orders to attack the convoy, but was repelled by the gunboat *Dato* and the bombardment of the SM.81s and later by the last Ju-52s to arrive in Tetuán. Finally, the destroyer was forced to withdraw to Málaga. This convoy was known as the 'Convoy of Victory' due to the importance of the number of men and materiel transported to the Iberian Peninsula.

By 9 August the Spanish airmen and sailors had carried four banderas and six tabores to Andalusia, which had already reached the gates of Mérida. The German Ju 52s then carried another 11 battalions (two banderas and nine tabores).

It is thus estimated that the number of men and kilos of materiel transported by air from 20 July to the beginning of November was as shown in Table 4.

Several 'regular' soldiers (*regulares*, North African troops in the service of Spain) wait to board a Ju 52 that will take them to the Iberian Peninsula during the airlift.

Table 4: Men and materiel transported by air

Month	Men	War Materiel (kg)
July	2,063	
August	8,453	104,000
September	9,732	248,670
October	2,300	17,290
November	845	

The main aircraft used in the airlift were three Fokker F.VII 3ms, two Dornier Wals, one DC-2, one Fokker V.VII, and 10 Ju 52s.

First Wartime Actions

Air hostilities began early, as the government ordered the bombing of Africa with Fokker F.VIIs, Douglas DC-2s and Breguet XIXs. However, shortly afterwards at Tablada, several of these aircraft, two F.VIIs and a DC-2, fell into the hands of the rebels. Three Ni52s that were undergoing repairs in Seville were captured by the rebels, who also managed to seize another three Republican Ni52s that landed in Granada, thinking that they were in the hands of the government.

Although it was not a combat shootdown, on the afternoon of 20 July, pilot Juan Antonio Ansaldo took off in his De Havilland 80 Puss Moth light aircraft from the Portuguese airport of Marinha, near Cascaes, with General José Sanjurjo, commander-in-chief of the rebel side, crashing into a fence and killing the latter. The pilot survived.

The numerous aircraft based in Madrid were used in the surrounding area, mainly controlling the nearby Guadarrama mountains, although some aircraft were deployed to Guipúzcoa, Asturias, Andalusia and Extremadura. The Barcelona Air Force set up an advanced base in Sariñena (Zaragoza) and used its seaplanes in air support for the landings in Ibiza and Mallorca; it mobilised 25 civilian pilots from the Catalan Aero-Clubs, who provided important war services. Los Alcázares and San Javier operated against Albacete and on the Granada and Teruel fronts.

A Breguet XIX at its base in Sariñena (Huesca). Noteworthy is the support vehicle with the *Alas Rojas* (Red Wings) emblem. The squadron based there was the first of the Republicans to mark its aircraft with red bands for proper identification of its own and enemy aircraft.

For the Nationalists, the Northern Air Force had the Breguet XIXs from Logroño and León, the Breguet XIXs that escaped from Getafe and El Prat and those that arrived in Burgos from the south (four Nieuport 52s, seven Breguet XIXs and two Fokker F.VIIs). A Breguet patrol was sent from Logroño to Zaragoza, as a counterweight to the aircraft from Sariñena. The Breguets and Nieuport from Tablada and Armilla and the aeroplanes of the Aero Club of Andalusia acted in defence of Córdoba, Granada and Seville and in support of the columns in the South. With the Dornier Wal from Cádiz and three Savoia S.62s from Marín, a mixed squadron of naval aviators was created.

Crew members of a Savoia S.62 belonging to the rebel side with a Popeye painted on the bow and General Mola's name on the fuselage.

A Nieuport Ni.52 belonging to the rebel side. This aircraft was the main fighter at the beginning of the SCW, soon to be replaced by German and Italian aircraft.

A Republican Breguet XIX with its red insignia in flight over the Central Operations Front.

The first shootdowns of the conflict occurred only a few days after it began. On the Republican side, the first shootdown was attributed to Captain Manuel Cascón on 20 July flying a Ni52 against a Breguet XIX, although this was not confirmed. On the rebel side, the first downing of an aircraft was by Lieutenant Bermúdez de Castro on 23 July, when he shot down a Republican Ni52 over Andújar with his Ni52 captured at the Armilla air base in Granada. The rebel lieutenant Miguel Guerrero also shot down a Dornier Wal from Granada on 25 July and later a Vickers Vildebeest on 29 July, a Breguet XIX on 1 August and two more Vickers Vildebeests.

With this large number of shootdowns in eastern Andalusia, the Republican air force based at the nearby base at Los Alcázares (Murcia) began to harass the area of Granada, leaving the air bridge between North Africa and the south of the Iberian Peninsula free of Republican fighters.

The first recorded combat between a plane from each side with their new insignia took place over Loja, in Granada, on 12 August. The plane shot down was a Republican Vickers Vildebeest based in Los Alcázares, that was trying to bomb the Nationalist troops advancing on Málaga; and the victorious plane was a Ni52 piloted by what was to be the greatest aviation ace during the SCW: Joaquín García Morato. This Nationalist pilot was the top Spanish aerobatic ace and only a few days earlier had been in Great Britain taking part in an air rally, managing to reach Spain within a few days of the start of the SCW.

A Republican Breguet XIX being prepared for the next flight possibly at Alcalá de Henares (Madrid).

Superb photograph of a Republican Breguet XIX in flight. The red bands on both wings and the cockade on the lower wing can be seen.

One of the 50 or so Nieuport 52C.1s that remained in the hands of the Republicans at the start of the SCW.

One of the Republican Nieuport 52C.1s in flight over Castellón in October 1937.

The first fighter pilots of the rebel side used the few Ni52C.1s available, with which such outstanding pilots as the aforementioned Captain Joaquín García Morato, Captain Ángel Salas Larrazábal shot down a light aircraft over the Teruel area on 23 August, Lieutenant Miguel García Pardo shot down a Br. XIX over the Guadarrama mountains on 9 August, Lieutenant Miguel Guerrero García who shot down a Dornier Wal, two Vickers Vildebeest and a Br. XIX over the Strait of Gibraltar on 25 July, Lieutenant Narciso Bermúdez de Castro who shot down a Ni52C.1 on 27 July over Piñar, in Granada, and Lieutenant Julio Salvador Benjumea-García who shot down a Ni52C.1 over the Madrid mountains on 28 July. Despite the good use they made of this aircraft, in September 1936 with the arrival of the more advanced CR.32 and He 51, the Spanish pilots exchanged their mounts for the new planes.

Also, in the first weeks of the war, bombing actions began to be carried out beyond their own lines on targets considered to be of interest. This was the case on 15 and 28 August and 3 and 22 September 1936 over the naval base at Ferrol, which was in the hands of the rebel side and where the cruisers *Baleares* and *Canarias* were being built. In the first three cases a DC-2 was used and in the fourth a Potez 54. The anti-aircraft defence at the naval base was minimal and only with the arrival on 16 August of the cruiser *Almirante Cervera* was artillery available against the attackers as the two cruisers under construction were not yet armed.

Aircraft Initially Purchased by Both Sides

The need to increase the air forces of both sides was evident from the first days after the coup d'état. Both the Republican government and the Nationalist rebels began the arduous task of procuring almost every type of aircraft available in Europe to take part in the conflict. The Republican government as early as 19 July asked for help from France – when the government had already bombed the rebels at Ceuta and Tetouan – by telegram requesting planes and weapons. The French government with León Blum as prime minister, was sympathetic to the Spanish government, and agreed the next day that France would help the Madrid government. On the 22nd, the Spanish ambassador in Paris requested 20 Potez 54s and weapons of all kinds, and although León Blum agreed at first, he finally had to allow it, not as the French government but through private, unofficial transactions, and therefore the planes that were sold would be unarmed.

Once the Spanish money began to arrive in France (sent from 30 July by two LAPE DC-2s), more combat-ready aircraft began to arrive. On 8 August, 13 Dewoitine D.37 fighters were delivered between 7 and 9 August (of which a total of 40 would arrive) and six twin-engine Potez 54s (of which 50 would arrive before the end of 1936) that would constitute the main Republican bombing force, as well as between 30 and 35 Marcel Bloch 200 and 210s. The Potez bomber will be referred to here as the Potez 54, although depending on their variants they were called Potez 540 or Potez 542 for example. The shipment of weapons to Spain was so complicated that for example the Dewoitine D.37s arrived unarmed (they came from a shipment that was to be sent to Lithuania) and a pair of 7.7mm machine guns had to be mounted on the wings. Thirty-six D-37s formed the so-called 2nd Laffayette Squadron or *Deuxiéme Lafayette*, flown by foreign volunteers and Spanish pilots. These French-made fighters would be the spearhead of the FARE until October 1936, when practically none remained in flight due to their heavy use and attrition.

Other aircraft that gradually arrived for the Spanish government were two Dewoitine D.510s (disassembled and the engines of both aircraft were returned to France), six Loire 46s flown by Malraux's volunteers between 3 and 7 September (of an order for 20 aircraft that were never delivered), seven Bristol Bulldog Mk.II (possibly from Estonia), 34 Potez 25s (25 from France and nine purchased by the Basque government from Latvia) and some 10 Gourdou Lesseure GL.32s (from France).

As can be seen, the arrival of aircraft on the Republican side was short and many different models were generally obsolete. In spite of this, it was thanks to the initial help from France that the Republican air force did not give up its efforts against the Nationalist air force, supported by modern German and Italian aircraft that were taking control of the Spanish skies.

The two D.510s finally received new engines (Soviet-built M-100s) and were commissioned in 1937 for the El Carmolí Fighter School and later the 71st Group.

A Dewoitine D.371 with the insignia of the Republican side at San Javier aerodrome.

Several Republican crewmen pose in front of a Dewoitine D.510 at San Javier.

These planes from France were a small help to the Republican government, but it seemed insufficient as French industry could not afford to deliver more planes. Many countries were approached to sell armaments of all kinds, one of the most important being Poland. Faced with this situation, however, the main European countries, led by France, signed a 'Non-Intervention Agreement in Spain'. The idea was initially conceived by the French government when, at the end of July 1936, it discovered that the Italian government was helping the rebels. Faced with the choice of whether to help either side or not, it was decided that its position would be one of non-intervention. The French government thus closed the border with Spain on 13 August. After France, Britain immediately joined the French proposal.

Just a few days later, at the end of August 1936, all the European states (except the neutral Switzerland) followed in the footsteps of France and Britain and signed the 'Agreement on Non-Intervention in Spain' in which they decided to 'strictly abstain from any direct or indirect interference in the internal affairs of that country' and prohibited 'the export... re-export and transit to Spain, Spanish possessions or the Spanish zone of Morocco, of all kinds of arms, munitions and war materiel'. To formalise and enforce this agreement, the Non-Intervention Committee was set up in London on 9 September, on which all the major European powers were represented, including Germany, Italy and the Soviet Union.

This agreement in principle showed the firm European decision not to take sides in the war in Spain, thus considering the Republican and rebel sides on the same level of legitimacy.

Although the Non-Intervention Agreement in Spain was presented as a firm European response to the war there, the reality was quite different, as countries such as Italy, Germany and Portugal, which had already begun selling and sending arms to Spain (to the rebel side), continued to do so despite signing the Agreement. In fact, Italy and Germany were the two main suppliers of all types of armaments to the rebel side throughout the war. Proof of this policy on the part of Italy and Germany was that at the end of August (almost at the same time as they signed the Agreement on Non-Intervention in Spain), the heads of the German and Italian military secret services (Admiral Wilhelm Canaris and General Mario Roatta, respectively) met in Rome to 'continue, despite the arms embargo, supplies of war materiel and munitions deliveries, in accordance with General Franco's requests'.

Despite Europe's good intentions, there were too many interests at both the national and European arms industry levels to pass up such a good opportunity to profit from Spain's war.

Despite the Agreement of Non-Intervention in Spain, simultaneously with the movements of the rebels, the Republican side would also continue to receive armaments from European countries, most notably the Soviet Union, which from October 1936 began to send modern armaments to the Republican side after denouncing to the League of Nations that the rebel side was receiving armaments from Italy and Germany (which was completely true).

For its part, the rebel side also began to make efforts abroad to obtain materiel of all kinds, including aircraft, of course. At the time of the coup d'état, the rebel side had its forces divided between the northern part of the country and North Africa, with a considerable distance between the two areas. As a result, two different diplomatic missions from the rebel side were sent to Europe to obtain armaments. One was sent by General Franco, leader of the rebels after the death of General Sanjurjo on 20 July, and the other by General Mola. The first diplomatic delegation was led by Luis Antonio Bolín, while the second was led by Pedro Sáinz, Goicoechea and Zunzunegui.

On 19 July Bolín left in a Dragon Rapide for Rome, with a stopover in Biarritz, to request fighters, bombers and bombs at the direction of General Sanjurjo, and later Franco. A few days later, on 24 July, the other rebel delegation arrived in Rome with Goicoechea at its head with the same requests. The result was Mussolini's yes to send 12 modern Savoia SM.81 bombers to the rebels. These aircraft took off on 30 July from Elmas, at Cagliari in Sardinia, under the command of Colonel Ruggero Bonomi for Melilla, but three of them did not arrive for various reasons (one landed in French Morocco, another landed in Algeria and the third crashed in the sea), so only nine arrived in Spanish Morocco where they quickly entered service.

On the afternoon of 23 July, a *Lufthansa* Junkers Ju 52 with registration number D-APOL took off for Germany, taking off that day and spending the night in Seville. On board were Johannes Bernhardt, who worked for the firm H. O. Wilmer, a supplier to the Spanish Army, and the head of the Nazi party in Morocco, Adolf P. Langenheim. The Spanish delegate Arranz requesting military aid from Adolf Hitler. On 25 July, despite initial reluctance, Adolf Hitler agreed to provide the 10 Junkers Ju 52s requested (necessary for the passage of troops from North Africa through the Strait of Gibraltar to the Iberian Peninsula), to which he added a further 10, bringing the total to 20. The code name for the operation to deliver arms to the rebels was Operation Magic Fire (*Unternehmen Zauberfeuer*). Hitler was to obtain from the Spaniards, among other things, an advantageous deal for strategic materials such as tungsten, although Spain would also later be used as a testing ground for the *Luftwaffe*.

Simultaneously with the arrival of the SM.81s in Spain, a Junkers Ju 52, flown by *Flugkapitan* Hencke, of *Lufthansa*, arrived from Germany in Spanish Morocco. This was the first of the 20 aircraft that Hitler had agreed to supply to the Nationalist side. This aircraft immediately began to participate in the airlift over the Strait of Gibraltar. The remaining 19 Ju 52s would arrive by air from Dessau in Germany, except for D-AMYN, the crew of which became confused and tried to land at Barajas, but instead landed at Azuaga,

The Dragon Rapide was an important liaison aircraft used by both sides. The one in the picture belongs to the rebel side.

The Ju 52s were, after their initial use as bombers, important transport aircraft for the rebel side.

where it was captured by the Republicans. In addition to the air shipments, a merchant ship called *Usaramo* also carried a variety of materiel. This ship, from the *Afrikalinien Hamburg* shipping line, left Hamburg on 31 July for Cádiz carrying six Heinkel He 51 fighter planes, 10 Junkers Ju 52s, 20 anti-aircraft guns, communications equipment and ammunition. In addition, 86 German soldiers, mainly from the *Luftwaffe* under the command of Major Von Scheele, who travelled under the guise of a group of German Work Front tourists, travelled as military advisors with orders to instruct the Spaniards in the handling of the equipment and not to intervene directly in the fighting except in the event of being attacked. The six pilots for the He 51s were Eberhard (who would achieve seven victories in Spanish skies), Knüppel (eight victories), Trautloft (five victories), von Houwald (five victories), Klein (one victory) and Hefter (one victory).

After the He 51s were assembled in Tablada (Seville), they began to be used as fighters with success as they were superior to the Ni52s, although the forthcoming arrival of modern aircraft from the Soviet Union would relegate them to assault duties. But despite rapid training in the piloting of this aircraft, as the Spanish pilots did not adapt to the aircraft, a number of accidents occurred, which meant that the German pilots, commanded by Lieutenant Eberhard, ended up taking part in the fighting. Despite this, on 18 August García Morato and Julio Salvador, forming part of what was officially called the Spanish Fighter Squadron, shot down a Potez 54, a Br. XIX and an Ni52C.1 with their He 51s.

On 23 August, six disassembled Heinkel He 46C-1s arrived in Lisbon on the ship *Kamerun*. They were transferred to Seville by rail and began flying in September 1936. Together with nine that arrived in October, three squadrons of six aircraft were formed with Spanish crews, named 1-E-11, 2-E-11 and 3-E-11.

For their part, the Italians began to send more war materiel after the SM.81s. In this case, the first Fiat CR.32 fighters, which were already the standard fighters of Italian aviation, began to arrive in mid-August. There were 12 Fiat CR.32s that arrived on the merchant ship *Nereide* from La Spezia to Melilla on 14 August 1936. These fighters, together with the nine SM.81s that had arrived a few days earlier, formed the basis of the Tercio's Aviation. On the *Nereide*, 18 volunteers from the *Regia Aeronautica* also arrived in Spain with false passports, 12 of whom were pilots, and spare parts for the planes. In command of this group was Captain Vincenzo Dequal of the *1° Stormo Caccia Terrestre*. All the Italian volunteers enlisted in the Spanish Legion (known as the *Tercio de Extranjeros*) with their equivalent ranks. These men belonging to the Italian *Regia Aeronautica* were assembled by Duke Amadeo d'Aosta at the Gorizia airfield in August 1936 to recruit them for a 'risky mission in Spain'.

As the aircraft came disassembled, they had to be assembled in Nador, after which they were flown to the Tablada aerodrome, officially forming the 1st Fighter Squadron of the Tercio Aviation (also known as the *Dequal* Squadron and later known as the *Cucaracha*). The arrival of these agile Italian biplanes swung the air battle in favour of the rebel side.

These 12 CR.32s were only the first of approximately 400 that would arrive in Spain from Italy over the next two and a half years, as well as some 600 Italian pilots, all under the name *Operazioni Militari Spagna* (Military Operations in Spain). In October, a batch of 12 CR.32s arrived to further dominate the Spanish skies. The imports of the first weeks, both Italian and German, allowed the rebel side to achieve air superiority, albeit with great effort.

Apart from France, for the Republican side, and Germany and Italy for the Nationalist side, another country that made significant profits in arms sales to both sides was Poland. The following is a brief account of the start of Spanish-Polish relations at the beginning of the SCW.

The Italian merchant ship *Nereide*, which after unloading armaments in the port of Melilla (from La Spezia) was stopped on 16 August 1936 by the Republican submarine C-2, although the presence of the Italian destroyer *Antonio da Noli* allowed the ship to continue its journey.

In the early days of the war in Spain, José Giral as president of the Council of Ministers of the Republican government requested through the Polish embassy in Madrid the purchase of 15 fighters of the PZL P.11 or the more modern PZL P.24 model. This official request was sent to Poland, where it was not received with much interest, although neither did it receive a refusal in response. In practice, the Polish government put various obstacles in the way of facilitating the sale of the aircraft. The main reason given by the Polish government was the low production of these aircraft models, in addition to the technical difficulties that such a sale would have due to the signing of the Non-Intervention Agreement in Spain.

Faced with the Polish refusal, the Spanish government's response was to increase the value of the order by adding ammunition for the aircraft and, of course, the intention to pay in gold and not in other currencies.

But despite breaking the legality established in the Agreement on Non-Intervention in Spain, the Polish government saw the situation in the Spanish war as a good opportunity to sell, to both the Republican and rebel sides, a large amount of obsolete military equipment in Polish warehouses and arsenals, much of it from the First World War. In addition to getting rid of these weapons, the Polish government would also be able to renew the Polish Army's armaments, thus obtaining a double benefit. In addition to getting rid of these weapons, the inflow of large sums of money would make it possible to renew the Polish Army's armaments, thus achieving a double benefit. At the same time, the Polish arms companies would be able to increase their production again, as the Polish government itself would be their main customer. Evidently, due to the impossibility of such a legal arms trade, many intermediaries were willing to carry out such transactions, possibly allowing some Polish military officials and politicians to make a lot of money from them, although this is difficult to prove.

The chaotic situation in Spain when the war began in 1936 meant that, in addition to the request for arms from the Madrid government, regional governments such as that of Catalonia also tried to obtain arms by their own means. As early as the first days of August 1936, the Ministry of Defence of the *Generalitat de Catalunya* (regional government of Catalonia) commissioned Major Alfredo Sanjuán Colomer and the industrial engineer Fernando Cuito

Canals to undertake a special mission to various European countries in order to acquire armaments. Czechoslovakia and Poland were their destinations on their trip due to the important arms industry in both countries.

On 10 August the Spanish delegation arrived in Prague and landed in Warsaw three days later. There they were received by Lieutenant Colonel Wladyslaw Sokolowski, the director of SEPEWE (*Syndykat Eksportu Przemysłu Wojennego*, War Industries Export Syndicate), and the envoys from Catalonia raised the need for various types of armaments for the Republican side. The urgent need to acquire weapons prompted the Spaniards to offer to buy immediately at least 10 TK-3 tanks, 500 light and 500 heavy machine guns, 20,000 hand grenades and eight million rounds for the machine guns. However, aware of the illegality of arms sales by European countries to Spain, they suggested to SEPEWE the possibility of sending the weapons to Spain, but through an order placed by the government of a third country, in this case Uruguay. All the documentation had to be signed by the Uruguayan government and payment would be made through a French bank account by the South American country, while the payment would go out through a French bank that would present it as coming from Uruguay. Following the Spanish proposal, SEPEWE representatives contacted the Polish Ministry of Foreign Affairs to discuss the possibility of carrying out the arms sale.

Another delegation, sent in this case by the Republican government in Madrid in mid-August, also had Warsaw on its route plan, after passing through Berlin, arriving on 18 August. There the Spanish envoy, Air Force Lieutenant Colonel Luis Riaño Herrero, who as head of the Military Aviation training service, had on his agenda the acquisition of armaments in several countries.

In one way or another, using various countries in the Americas, such as Mexico and Uruguay, as official buyers of armaments of various kinds, ships loaded with rifles, machine guns, ammunition, hand bombs, gunpowder, etc. began to sail from the port of Danzig from 9 September 1936. At this time the arms dealers began to do their work, selling their huge stocks of armaments, in many cases from the First World War. From that time on, many ships loaded with military equipment left the Polish port of Gdynia and the port of the free city of Danzig from September and November 1936.

For its part, the rebel side did not take long to contact the Polish government with the same aim as the Republican side. Thus, on Sunday 11 October 1936, Santiago Muguiro (secretary of the Spanish embassy in London) and Major Carmelo de las Morenas (aeronautical attaché in Paris and London) arrived in Warsaw from London with the aim of acquiring some £69,000 worth of war materiel for the rebels. Major Carmelo de las Morenas established contact with SEPEWE, which acted as an intermediary company for the Polish government.

The Spanish rebel delegation proposed to make the purchase through a third country, in this case Portugal, which was not affected by the arms embargo proposed for the contenders by the London Non-Intervention Committee. It was finally possible to acquire 20 PWS-10 fighters and four RWD-13 liaison aircraft (the latter were sold directly to Spain according to SEPEWE archives). The former were in such poor condition that they had to be completely overhauled and were put into service at the CWL workshops in Dęblin before being shipped by SEPEWE.

For various reasons, the purchase was delayed, and Juan Serrat – representative of the rebels in Poland – assumed that it was because of the agent who mediated the transaction, Stefan Czarnecki, also

In January 1937 three RWD-13 liaison aircraft purchased in Poland were landed in the port of Vigo. In Spain they were known as *Polacas* (Polish).

The rebel side received four RWD-13s which were used as liaison aircraft throughout the conflict. They carried the military designation 30-1 to 30-4. The Morato Group was assigned one of these aircraft. One of these aircraft at Valenzuela airfield.

At the end of 1936, 15 Polish PWS-10 aircraft were secretly sold to the rebel side through the Spanish ambassador in Paris. The need for aircraft forced the purchase of many that were obsolete, as was the case here.

Nice photograph of the PWS-10 *Chiquita* preparing for its next flight. These aircraft were so antiquated and so full of defects that they were considered unsuitable for combat and therefore destined for training and use at the Conversion School then based at El Copero, not far from Seville.

The PWS-10 were slowly withdrawn from service and stored in the Southern Regional Park. By the end of 1938 none of them remained in service and their time in rebel service was over.

worked for the Republican government. Stefan did not hesitate to put various obstacles in the way of the rebel side's orders while favouring the orders of the Republican side. Despite this, the rebels managed to buy the planes from Poland, which the Republican government did not.

First Combat With New Aircraft of German, French and Italian Origin

As the Italian and German planes arrived, the Republic's aviation lost the opportunity to intercept the troops flying through the Strait of Gibraltar in slow, poorly armed transport planes that would have been easily shot down by the Ni52 fighters. Instead, the Republican aviation concentrated on the Madrid area, as well as on Los Alcázares.

Some of the most renowned Squadrillas of the Republican side included the 'Circus Krone' Squadron (a name not used during the war, the correct one being Aviation in the Northern Air Zone) which owed its name to the disparity and variety of aircraft models, including the Breguet XIX, Bristol Bulldog Mk.II, Gourdou Lesseurre GL.32, Potez 25, Letov S.321, and Ni52. This unit, which as can be seen from its aircraft, was hastily organised, operated mainly in the Northern zone. The initial mission of these aircraft was reconnaissance and light bombing. As can be imagined, the large number of mostly obsolete aircraft models meant that it suffered heavy attrition and a high number of casualties during the fighting on the Northern front.

Another, the 'Spain' Squadron was composed of international volunteers (from French to White Russians and various other European nationalities) who participated and fought in the SCW for pay. It was organised by André Malraux and was therefore also known as the 'Malraux' Squadron. This unit, equipped with

Nieuport 52C.1s like this one with Republican insignia were the most abundant fighters on the Republican side at the start of the SCW.

An old-fashioned Hispano DH.9 belonging to the rebel side. With the arrival of new aircraft from Germany and Italy, these pre-war aircraft were relegated to secondary duties.

Potez 54 bombers and Dewoitine fighters, operated over Badajoz on 14 August (meeting six Ju 52s in the air) and had some success in holding off the rebel troops advancing towards Extremadura. They also participated in assisting Republican ground attacks on Córdoba, where they were engaged by three CR.32s. The writer and politician André Malraux recruited international volunteers for his squadron, but mainly French, who in many cases were mercenaries attracted by the 50,000 francs a month they were paid. This squadron operated between August 1936 and March 1937, which was when the contracts of the international unit's pilots came to an end. Throughout their service they suffered numerous casualties.

The '*Alas Rojas*' (Red Wings) Squadron was based in Sariñena. This unit was the first to use the red insignia worn by Republican aircraft until the end of the SCW. Its area of operations was mainly the Aragón region, dominating the skies of the area until the arrival of Italian and especially German aircraft.

It is important to remember the foreign participation in the war in Spain before the arrival of Italian, German and Soviet aid in large quantities. On the Republican side, many pilots joined the FARE, as was the case of a group of British pilots who arrived in Spain in September 1936 to support the Republic. Some of these pilots, including Vincent P.J. Doherty, Brian D. Griffin, Charles Kennet, John Wilson, Patrick J.H. Mertz, Claude Warsow, Edward A.J. Hillman, Keith O.D. Lindsay, Edward Downes-Martin and Eric Griffiths, had military experience from the Royal Air Force Reserve. Most of these volunteers manned Breguet XIXs and Ni52C.1s, fighting first on the Central Front and later in the Spanish Levante. By early 1937 almost none of them were still in service, Downes-Martin, Griffin and Warsow having been shot down, while Griffiths and Wilson were wounded in action.

Later, apart from the Soviet pilots, of course, there was also another country that contributed a small number of pilots, namely the United States. At a difficult time in the USA, several pilots served in the FARE. The two most prominent and who went on to become great pilots were Frank Tinker who achieved eight victories including a Bf 109A while flying an I-16, and Albert Baumler with four confirmed victories, a fifth shared victory and two probable victories. The behaviour of the rest of his comrades was mixed, with some eventually switching sides after being captured and others causing various incidents due to poor discipline.

After their arrival in Spain, the He 51s began their missions flown by the Spanish pilots Rambaud, García Pardo, Salvador, García Morato and Ramiro Pascual – in the squadron popularly known as the Rambaud Squadron – from the middle of August onwards, with García Morato and Salvador each achieving two shootdowns on the 18th. Unfortunately, two of the planes suffered accidents, which served as an excuse for the German pilots who had come with the Heinkels to ask to be allowed to carry out war missions. The German help was very important and they did not want any confrontations with them, so Kindelán, the recently appointed chief general of the Air Services, agreed that only the Germans would fly the He 51s, dispersing the Spanish pilots. In just a couple of weeks, the German He 51 pilots managed to shoot down six enemy aircraft, although they also shot down a Nationalist Dragon Rapide.

Once the air bridge was channelled, six Ju 52s left it to form under the command of von Moreau two bombing squadrons called *Pedro* and *Pablo*. Eventually, three Spanish squadrons were formed, which were included in Squadron B, which with German crews supported the capture of Mérida and Badajoz, bombed Cuatro Vientos, Getafe, Barajas and supported the defence of the Alcázar of Toledo and the capture of San Sebastián and Irún. Each of the two German squadrons had three Ju 52/3m prepared as bombers (*behelfsbomber*), with *Pedro* under the command of *Oberleutnant* von Moreau and *Pablo* under the command of *Oberleutnant* Joester. On 10 August, nine Ju 52s began to operate over Extremadura where they would encounter aircraft from the Republican *España* Squadron. Von Moreau with a Ju 52/3m fitted as a *behelfsbomber*, on 13 August bombed the Republican battleship *Jaime I* in the vicinity of Málaga, hitting it with five 300kg bombs, causing a large number of dead and wounded, forcing the battleship to take refuge in the port of Cartagena. On the 20th, von Moreau and Henke with Spanish B Squadron moved to the San Fernando airfield (Salamanca) to support operations in Asturias. The third Ju 52 squadron, created in August 1936, was given the name of the *Three Marys* (its three aircraft being named: *María Magdalena*, *María Cruz* and *María de la O*, after three fashionable songs of the time). This 3rd Squadron (3-E-22) would later become the 4th Squadron (4-E-22).

Ju 52s and He 51s piloted by Spaniards bombed Madrid airfields on 23 August, and this attack was answered with Potez 54s and Dewoitines on 26 August against Olmedo airfield and on 30 August against Escalona airfield.

In just a few days after their arrival, at the end of July, the first 12 Italian CR.32s began operations with patrols and solo missions, suffering several mishaps. It was not until 21 August 1936 that the first enemy aircraft was shot down, a Ni52 shot down over Córdoba by Lieutenant Ugo Ceccherelli. A few days later, Sergeant Magistrini claimed another Ni52 shot down near Granada. These first victories of the little Fiat were the beginning of a successful service record for this aircraft in Spain, although at the end of 1936, with the arrival of Soviet-made aircraft, it lost its hegemony in the air.

The 3rd Ju 52 squadron in flight. In the background can be seen the aircraft christened *María Magdalena* (written on the tail) and with the name *Trechuelo* on the fuselage.

On 3 September another nine CR.32s arrived with their Italian pilots and technicians, forming the 2nd Fighter Squadron of the Tercio Aviation under the command of Captain Dante Olivera.

Despite the increasing successes with the CR.32, Colonel Bonomi was aware that the use of aircraft alone, in pairs or trios was not appropriate, believing that their use in large numbers would allow maximum use to be made of the fighters. Eventually, this thinking evolved into the creation of a Squadron composed of the 19 or 20 fighters available under Dequal's command. With the arrival of more CR.32s, a 3rd Fighter Squadron was formed (the three squadrons were part of the so-called Gruppo Caccia di Torrijos).

As happened on the rebel side, the first battles led to structural changes in aviation. In fact, in September the Republic reorganised aviation, integrating it into the new Ministry of the Navy and Air Force, unifying Military, Naval and Civil Aviation.

Shipments of war materiel continued on both sides, even in limited quantities, as in the case of the Hs 123. In the second week of September, two Henschel Hs 123 dive bomber aircraft arrived in the port of Cádiz on the German ship *Wigbert* (a Heinkel He 50G dive bomber aircraft also arrived, but there is no record that it was ever used), which were immediately sent to Tablada where they were assembled. They would be known as *Angelito* and from the end of October they would be incorporated into the Condor Legion together with four more aircraft of the same model. During December and the beginning of January 1937 from their base in Tablada they operated on the Andalusian front. Almost at the same time, on 14 September, the German ship *Eisenach* arrived in the port of Seville with various military equipment, including two Heinkel He 60D seaplanes, which were sent to Cádiz where they were later assembled. Another example is the three Junkers (W)34 that arrived in October from Germany, one of which was used by the Chief of the Southern Army, General Queipo de Llano, the other two serving in the Condor Legion.

In the second half of October, the He 60Ds from their base in Cádiz carried out coastal reconnaissance and attacks on the airfield of El Rompedizo (Málaga) where some Republican Breguet XIX and Vickers Vildebeest were based. Specifically, on 15 October, the two He 60Ds made a very destructive attack on the Málaga airfield. The following day, the He 60D shot down one Breguet XIX.

As for the Breguet XIXs on the rebel side, in October they were reorganised into 10 squadrons, of three aircraft each, in five Groups: 1-G-10 in Logroño, 2-G-10 in León, 3-G-10 in Seville, 4-G-10 in Granada and 5-G-10 in North Africa.

In October 1936, three He 51 B-1s were acquired from Germany with funds obtained popularly in Aragón and were therefore 'baptised' as *Zaragoza*, *Huesca* and *Teruel*, which together with three more received in September formed two squadrons that were generally used on secondary fronts, since with the arrival of the CR.32s, the latter were used on the main fronts due to their superiority.

There was also a short bombing campaign over Cartagena and Los Alcázares during October 1936 by the Nationalist side. On 18 October two Ju.52/3m from the *Pedros* and *Pablos* squadrons, with German crews, were deployed at Armilla from where they took off to reach Cartagena and dropped 10 bombs of 250kg each against the ships anchored at the dock, without being damaged by the anti-aircraft artillery. On 20 October three Ju 52/3m of the Spanish squadrons (1-E-22 and 2-E-22) bombed Cartagena again with six bombs of 250kg each. On 27 October three SM.81s of the Tercio Aviation bombed the base at Los Alcázares (where the I-15, I-16 and SB-2s would be assembled) while five Ju 52/3m attacked the port of Cartagena.

On 9 October, 10 IMAM Romeo Ro.37bis arrived in Vigo, forming two squadrons, 1-E-12 (commanded by Spanish Captain Muñoz Jiménez Jiménez) and 2-E-12 (commanded by Italian Captain Colacicchi).

A pair of dive attack Hs 123s that joined VJ/88.

One of the Hs 123 known as *Angelito* used in the SCW on ground attack duties.

A Heinkel He 60 from the Nationalist side after an accident at its base.

Fights for Ibiza and Mallorca

After the SCW began, only Menorca in the Balearic Islands remained loyal to the Republican government. But a plan was soon drawn up to regain control of the rebel islands, so that as early as 8 August Catalan and Valencian government forces seized Ibiza almost without a fight, thanks to air captain Alberto Bayo, who succeeded with a requisitioned ship, two destroyers, a submarine and six seaplanes. The rebel forces on Mallorca were few in number, and on 16 August forces from Barcelona and Menorca consisting of some 8,000 men landed on the east of the island, establishing a large beachhead with the support of the Navy and S.62 and M.18 seaplanes from Mahón and Barcelona, which dominated the skies for 11 days.

The SM.81s were the first modern bombers to fly in the SCW. They formed the *Grupo 28* consisting of two Italian squadrons attached to the Tercio Aviation.

A Savoia S.62 seaplane participating in the Bayo expedition, an attempt by the Republican side to conquer the islands of Mallorca and Ibiza held by the rebels in August-September 1936).

This Tupolev SB-2 prepares to take-off from La Senia airfield along with other aircraft with their engines running.

A Savoia S.62 from the Hydroplane School at the Los Alcázares base in 1937.

Savoia S.62 seaplanes played an important role in the rebels' air forces in their fight for control of the sea.

Thanks to the resistance of the rebels, six aircraft were sent to Palma de Mallorca on 27 August by ship: three Fiat CR.32s (which formed the Mussolini Squadron) and three Macchi M.41 seaplanes. Immediately afterwards, three Savoia SM.81s were sent, in this case flying on 28 August. Thanks to the reinforcements, the Republican troops were finally defeated, having to withdraw, leaving three S.62s and a Macchi M.18 abandoned on the beachhead and causing the Generalitat troops to reembark on 4 September (in their attempt to invade Mallorca). In these battles, a CR.32, piloted by test pilot Carestiato, damaged a Savoia S.62, which was carrying the expedition leader Captain Bayo, and killing the pilot, Freire.

The arrival of the Italian fighters in Mallorca was decisive in preventing the conquest of the island by the Republican troops.

The Tajo Valley Campaign and the Advance Towards Madrid

Once the provinces of Seville and Cádiz had been controlled, the Nationalist troops advanced northwards through Extremadura with the intention of uniting their two areas of control of Spanish territory (north and south), and after advancing towards Talavera de la Reina their objective was the capital: Madrid. The same advance of the troops was intended to rescue the Nationalist troops stationed in the Alcázar of Toledo from the siege to which they were being subjected.

Once Franco and Mola's troops were united (from the south they approached from Badajoz, while from the north they left from Salamanca to Cáceres), it was decided to continue towards Madrid through the Tagus valley.

The Nationalists took Mérida on 11 August with the support of three SM.81s, and Badajoz on 14 August after being bombed by a Ju 52. From there they began their advance towards Talavera de la Reina. But in the face of this advance the Republican air force increased its attacks in the sector. The Potez 54s attacked the troops approaching from the southwest and in the vicinity of the town of Medellín attacked another column of Nationalist troops on 14 and 16 August. The Potez 54s also targeted the Córdoba-Sevilla railway tracks and Córdoba itself, which was bombed on the 16th.

Specifically, the city of Córdoba, in the hands of the Nationalists, suffered an attack by Republican troops under the command of General Miaja, although fortunately for the Nationalists, on 18 August the first three CR.32s arrived in Seville, of those transported by sea to Melilla, to control the skies over Córdoba.

Fighting began to become more frequent, as on 31 August 1936 between Talavera de la Reina and Oropesa, where at an altitude of 3,000 metres, two CR.32s which had taken off from Cáceres to inspect the Getafe area, were attacked by a Hawker Spanish Fury (piloted by Andrés García Lacalle, who would become one of the main Republican pilots) and possibly accompanied by two Ni52s. The result was the shooting down of the two Italian planes, piloted by Lieutenant Monico (who died after jumping out of the burning fighter and being captured by Republican militiamen) and *Sergente* Castellani (who managed to escape after crashing his plane in the Villanueva de la Serena area). They were the first Italian casualties in the SCW (their comrades marked the fuselage of their planes with the words *Monico! Presente* as a posthumous tribute to the first Italian pilot shot down in the SCW). For these shootdowns, García Lacalle, Alonso Santamaría and Peña were promoted to ensigns. After the advance of the ground troops, the Nationalist CR.32s were deployed in Cáceres, closer to the centre of the country.

Italian pilots had great problems flying over an unknown country and with inadequate cartography. There were several cases of CR.32s that ended up landing by mistake in Portugal, after

Assembly of the first C.32s arriving from Italy in Melilla. From there they would be sent to the Iberian Peninsula, playing an important role in the aviation of the rebels.

Assembly of the CR.32s arriving on the Italian merchant ship Nereide. Italy's immediate assistance to the rebels was of great importance.

One of the three Spanish Furies that remained in the hands of the FARE (Air Forces of the Spanish Republic) at SAF-15 at La Rabasa.

their pilots became lost. This situation led the commander of the Italian contingent, Colonel Ruggiero Bonomi, after a meeting with Kindelán, to agree to the incorporation of Spanish Captain García Morato into his fighter group. The aim was for the Spanish pilot to command the Italian aircraft patrols due to his better knowledge of the terrain. García Morato began training with the Italians in his CR.32 on 6 September. Subsequently, Spanish pilots Ángel Salas, Julio Salvador and later García Pardo joined the Italian unit. Morato, Salas and Salvador were the first of a group of pilots who, after training in the CR.32 with the Italians, would establish a fighter unit manned entirely by Spanish pilots, the so-called 'Blue Patrol' within the XVI Italian Gruppo Caccia. The insignia of the now famous Blue Patrol was a bustard, a hawk and a blackbird on a white field with the motto *Vista, Suerte y al Toro* and is still used today by the 11th Wing of the Spanish Air and Space Force on its Eurofighters.

As mentioned above, most of the Republican air force remained in the Madrid area (Getafe). From there its Ni52s protected the bombing of the mountains and the Alcázar of Toledo, without attacking either the area of the Strait of Gibraltar (with the air bridge) or the columns of Nationalist troops that were in Valladolid and Pamplona. In fact, the planes from Getafe were fundamental in the surrender of the La Montaña barracks and the military installations at Campamento. The Republican air dominance was increased by the remoteness of the Nationalist airfields of Logroño, Burgos and León, which meant that the airfields of Olmedo and Escalona had to be set up in August, and Ávila in September, as well as Arévalo.

On 13 September a patrol led by García Morato and the Italian sergeants Baschirotto and Patriarca met in the air a patrol of Vickers Vildebeest belonging to the *Aeronautica Naval*, which had been stationed in Getafe from their base at Los Alcáceres to take part in the bombing of the Nationalist troops in the Talavera de la Reina area, escorted by two Ni52s. After the clash, the Republican pilots Urtubi and Colom were shot down, as well as the Italian Patriarca, who was captured on the ground. On 16 September García Morato again managed to shoot down two Potez 54 bombers (one victory shared with Baschirotto) near Navalcarnero (Madrid).

At the end of September two Loire 46C1s (both piloted by mercenaries; the British Edward Gawen and the Frenchman Maxime Hantz) as well as a Dewoitine D.372 (also piloted by a Frenchman named René Issard who at least saved his life) were shot down.

With the first four Potez and a civilian Junkers, the first bombing squadron was formed, based at the new civilian airport of Barajas and under the command of Joaquín Mellado, chief of operations of LAPE, the main Spanish airline, who was promoted to captain because he was a military pilot in the reserve.

Another Potez 54 of the *España* Squadron christened *Aquí te espero* (which together with a DC-2 had two days earlier bombed the cruiser *Canarias* with large bombs, without effect, during its sea trials in Ferrol) was shot down on 25 September 1936 by Captain Ángel Salas Larrazábal together with Baschirotto. The Republican bomber was carrying out a bombing mission in the Toledo area, but had no escort aircraft (the Loire 46 assigned to it suffered a breakdown and did not accompany it). Although four of the six crew members survived, it seems that they committed suicide when

A Dewoitine D.372 at Málaga airport in 1936, or at El Carmolí. We can see the raised fists, a typical salute of the Republican side.

they mistook the Republican militiamen who came to their aid for enemy troops.

On 26 September, the Republican Ensign Peña shot down a Ju 52 over the Alcázar of Toledo (this aircraft belonged to B Squadron and was manned by the Spaniards Eustaquio Ruiz de Alda, Ensign Jenaro Lucas, Sergeant César Ledesma-Ramos and Sergeant San Juan, who was the only one to save his life by parachuting). This aircraft and the Potez 54 shot down the previous day by Salas were the first two multi-engine aircraft destroyed in Spain in combat (previously some other multi-engine aircraft had been damaged but subsequently repaired).

On 28 September, of the 21 CR.32s that had arrived in the Peninsula, only seven were still flying and five were under repair. Nine had been shot down. Because the fighting continued in different sectors such as the south, where on 8 October the Italian Ensign Mantelli shot down a Ni52 near Granada and on the 9th he shot down another Ni52, possibly from the 1st Squadron of the 31st Group, in the area of Andújar (Jaén).

The Nationalist troops were losing strength as they advanced towards Madrid and Toledo, but Toledo (and the defenders of its Alcázar) was occupied on 28 September. In Madrid the Nationalists managed to occupy the Casa de Campo and the Ciudad Universitaria, and the front remained stagnant in that sector. The Nationalists carried out bombing raids over Madrid with SM.81s and Ju 52s, engaging the Republicans based in that sector. Even the only Boeing 281 based in Getafe, which had been fitted with machine guns, was used to defend the Spanish capital. During the advance towards Madrid, the Nationalist side had 15 He 51s.

The only Boeing 281 that participated in the SCW. At the start of the SCW, the Boeing demonstration aircraft (to compete with the Hawker Fury as the new Spanish fighter) that was in Madrid was confiscated by the Republican government and subsequently armed (model 281 was the unarmed version of the P-26).

Another nice picture of the Spanish Boeing 281. After being armed with two 7.7 mm Vickers machine guns, it took part in several fights until it was shot down in September 1936.

If at the end of September García Morato already had eight aerial victories, on 16 October he shot down another Loire 46C over Madrid and on 18 October two Breguet XIXs over Illescas, as well as some captive balloons in the area of the Casa de Campo (Madrid). The CR.32s piloted by Italians also managed to shoot down in that sector six Dewoitine 371s on 15 October. The fact was that since the arrival of the CR.32s in Spain, the Nationalists had achieved supremacy in the air during the month of October while the planes supplied by France to the Republican government were becoming scarce. The CR.32s had achieved supremacy in the air against obsolete aircraft, mainly of French origin, but in November 1938 the situation changed, as will be seen below.

From November of the same year, the squadrons of B Squadron already numbered four: 1st 'Sanjurjo' Squadron, 2nd 'Toledo' Squadron, 3rd 'Las tres Marías' Squadron and 4th Squadron. The 1st and 4th squadrons were combined to form the Night Bombardment Group and the 1st and 4th squadrons were given the names 1-E-22 and 2-E-22 respectively. While the 2nd Squadron was renamed 3-E-22 and the 4th Squadron was renamed 4-E-22. Two more squadrons were later formed with Ju 52/3m, the 5-E-22 'Barberán' and the 6-E-22 'Navarra'.

Although most of the fighting moved from one front to the other, a war of attrition continued in the Central sector, as can be seen by the participation of aircraft from the Night Bombardment Group, specifically on 17 November aircraft belonging to 3-E-22, attacked the Florida and del Rey bridges in Madrid. In December attacks were made on enemy positions in Navalmoral, damaging several Ju 52s.

On 10 November 1936 a Ju 52/3m, belonging to 1-E-22, piloted by Sergeant Ananías San Juan took off from Escalona airfield near Madrid and landed in Republican territory in Alcalá de Henares. He deserted, and the government side now flew a modern Ju 52 that had recently arrived from Germany. Although there were not many cases, there were several deserters, from both sides, who went over to the other side with their aircraft, in some cases even killing a crew member who did not agree with the desertion.

Secondary Theatres of Operation

At the same time as the fighting in the south and centre of the country, clashes between the two sides took place in northern Spain. On the Basque front, the FARE deployed Breguet XIXs from Getafe at the airfields of Lasarte (San Sebastián) and Lamiaco (Bilbao). For its part, the rebel side had six of the same Breguet XIXs based in Logroño and Burgos, which not only operated in the north of the country, but also in the Central sector.

A Dewoitine D.371 with Republican insignia. At the beginning of the SCW, 40 of these aircraft were sent by the French government to the Republican side.

At the beginning of the SCW, the Dewoitine D.371 became the most numerous French-made fighter used in Spain.

One of the few Nationalist Fiat CR.32s captured by the Republicans and sent to the Soviet Union for evaluation. The insignia of its new owners can be seen.

A captured Fiat CR.32, although still with the insignia of the rebel side, at the Manises airfield.

The Ju 52 'Navarra' belonging to the Night Bombing Group in a photograph taken in 1937.

Although this was a sector where aircraft were not used on a massive scale, two Nieuports and a Vickers Vildebeest were sent by the Republican side from Sariñena to Lamiaco as reinforcements on 16 September, where all the FARE fighter planes were concentrated on 17 August.

For its part, the Nationalist side increased its air fleet in the sector by deploying two Fokker F.VIIs (from the south of the country) and a F.XII in Logroño, allowing the six Breguet XIXs to be deployed at the Lacua airfield in Vitoria.

The number of aircraft involved in the Northern sector gradually increased. On 23 September two patrols of He 51s and the five Ju 52s that bombed Bilbao on 25 September (three German and two Spanish) arrived in Vitoria.

Further east, in Aragón, nine He 51s under the command of Kraft Eberhardt arrived in Zaragoza in mid-October from Barahona airfield (Soria). These He 51s attacked 10 enemy aircraft at Almudévar on the 19th, destroying a DH Dragon. On 19 October an engagement took place over Alcubierre (Huesca) where three He 51s, piloted by von Houwald, Strümpell and Henrici, engaged 13 FARE aircraft and managed to shoot down five of them without loss. Henrici claimed one Ni52, one Breguet XIX and one F.VII, while the other two pilots claimed one Ni52 each. The He 51s were later sent to Ávila and replaced by six He 46s.

In Asturias, the FARE based in Llanes attacked Oviedo, in the hands of the rebels, from 21 August. Due to this fact, the Nationalists deployed a Fokker F.XII and a squadron of Ju 52s in León. Five He 51s under the command of Hannes Trauloft also participated as escorts for the National Aviation (*Aviación Nacional*, AN) planes that supplied Oviedo from the air. On 3 and 4 October the six planes from Llanes again attacked Oviedo several times, and finally moved their base to Carreño airfield (between Gijón and Avilés). In response, in mid-October six He 51 fighters and eight Ju 52 trimotors arrived in León; they were joined by three SM.81s and three CR.32s, commanded by Salas Larrazábal, which took part in an attack on the Carreño airfield.

Between battles, new aircraft arrived in Spain, such as the first 10 Italian-made Ro.37s, which arrived by merchant ship in the port of Vigo on 29 September. Up to 76 of this aircraft type would arrive throughout the SCW.

The total number of FARE aircraft in the northern sector on 4 October 1936 was 16 aircraft and four Savoia S.62 seaplanes with bases at Sondica, Lamiaco, La Albericia, and Llanes/Carreño, while the National Aviation initially had 27 aircraft after the arrival of the six Italian-made aircraft.

With the advance of the rebel troops from Galicia to Oviedo supported by aircraft based in León, the front moves further east.

The Ju 52s, SM.81s, CR.32s and He 51s were withdrawn from León and were replaced by three He 46 and three Breguet XIXs that would form the 1-G-10 Group at that air base.

On the south-eastern front (eastern Andalusia), the FARE deployed approximately 14 aircraft and four seaplanes in Málaga on 1 September, to which must be added the base of the 1st Squadron of the 21st Group (with Breguet XIXs and Ni52s) in Andújar (Jaén). With the aircraft based at Andújar, the Republican government bombed the city of Córdoba (in Nationalist hands) every day from 7 to 15 September. On the Nationalist side in the south (AN del Sur) between Seville, Córdoba and Granada there were four Ni-52s and some 17 Breguet XIXs, which from 21 September were joined by some SM.81s and CR.32s. With these aircraft the AN defended the skies over Córdoba and was able to attack the Republican airfield at Andújar, as well as to support the Nationalist offensive in the province of Córdoba towards Peñarroya, which was captured on 13 October. In the combats against Andújar on 9 October, the CR.32s faced three Ni52s, shooting down one of them; although the AN in the south also accumulated losses (two Ni52s and five Breguet XIXs). The 12 surviving Breguet XIXs were later assigned to Groups 3-G-10 and 4-G-10.

German He 51 pilot Hannes Trautloft recalls an encounter in his diary that took place on 17 September:

> Over Santa Olalla we distinguished two Potez bombers flying back home, heading for Madrid. We stung up to them with full fumes. This time, as we attack I look back and sure enough with a steep dive a Devoitin swoops down on us, like a goshawk on its prey. I have just enough time to warn Eberhard and Knüppel, when the guy has already come within shooting distance. I turn round and fly straight at him. He realises that he hasn't succeeded in the surprise and doesn't accept the fight, but instead, with greater speed, returns to hover above our kette, some 500 metres higher up. However, it doesn't look like a hero is sitting in the aircraft, because as soon as the Red fighter sees me it slips away as fast as possible in the direction of Madrid. The man in the Devotitin, on the other hand, is a feisty lad. He knows that his machine is superior to ours. And he exploits that advantage skilfully. Orbiting continuously some 500 metres above our kette, he only waits for the most favourable moment to launch an attack on us. But we tread carefully. For a while neither of us do anything,

An airfield where several Condor Legion aircraft (one Ju 52 and several He 51s) rest.

while keeping it perfectly in sight. Finally, it looks too silly for us. We spread our kette wide, maybe that way we can lure the Red one down. And it actually works, it attacks Eberhardt. Knüppel and I immediately move in. When, from about 300 metres away, we let him have our machine gun bursts, he gives up on Eberhardt and takes off. We are firing steadily behind him. But his machine is too fast, we can't catch him. It's about time we got faster machines.

The Red government offered a sort of price for the head of each Spanish Nationalist plane shot down: 50,000 pesetas. So high a price, to tell the truth, we had not priced ourselves; we received all kinds of respect for our price. But the fact that the Red pilots need such an incentive to go into combat – otherwise the guys would not have offered the 50,000 pesetas – does not please us at all. It is not a comfortable thought to have enemies for whom combat is basically a professional activity.

The Soviet Surprise

After the success of the airlift in the Strait of Gibraltar and the initial air dominance of the rebel forces, the situation for the Republican government became very difficult. The fact that Germany and Italy were helping the Nationalists did not please the Soviet Union, so Stalin decided to intervene to help the Spanish Republic. Of course, the help was not for free, as in a short space of time a large amount of gold from the Bank of Spain was transferred to the Soviet Union as payment. As early as 27 August, Spanish-Soviet relations had been maintained for the purchase of military equipment. Even at the end of August it was known that Soviet pilots were stationed at the Getafe base in Madrid.

The first Soviet contingent arrived in Spain on 10 September on the merchant ship *Rostok* with mechanics and materiel to set up a factory to build Soviet aircraft in Spain. It was not long before the first Soviet merchant ship, *Bolshevik*, docked in Cartagena on 13 October with 13 disassembled Polikarpov I-15s. On the 16th, 12 I-15s were transhipped at sea to a Spanish merchant ship *Larramendi*. On the 23rd, six I-15s arrived in Alicante on the merchant ship *Georgi Dimitrov*. Between 15 and 21 October, 30 SB-2s arrived in the port of Cartagena. On 28 October 25 I-15s arrived on the *Lepin*, on 3 November the *Kursk* with 15 I-16s and on 4 November the *Blagoev* with 16 I-16s. In addition, they brought armaments, spare parts, and fuel. The first 31 SB-2-M-100s arrived on the ships *Stari Bolshevik*, *Kim* and *Volgoles* on 15, 19 and 21 October respectively. The disassembled aircraft had to be assembled in San Javier during the month of October.

Above: On 13 October 1936, the merchant ship *Bolshevik* landed 18 Polikarpov I-15s in the port of Cartagena. Together with 14 other aircraft that arrived later, they were transferred to Los Alcázares, where they were assembled and put into service.

Left: The first I-16s arrived in Spain in October 1936 and became the FARE's most powerful fighter during the SCW. The one in the photo was a Type 5.

The SB-2 was the standard medium bomber of the FARE. Russia sent 142 units in nine shipments, but only 92 were received, as 50 of the last shipment were left in the French zone and returned to the Soviet Union.

Once the first 25 I-15s were assembled, a 1st Squadron, of Group 12, was formed at El Soto near Algete (Madrid) under the command of Pavel Rigachov (alias Palancar) and a 2nd Squadron of I-15s at the Escuela de Caza de Alcalá de Henares (Madrid) commanded by Sergei Tarkhov (alias Antonio). Both squadrons were assigned to Group 12. The I-15s known as *chaika* (Russian for seagull) were known in Spain as *Chatos* (because of their similar sound and small engine size like a nose) on the Republican side, while when they were discovered by the Nationalists, the latter mistook them for the American Curtiss Sparrowhawk aircraft and so they were called 'Curtiss'. Later (as the I-15s arrived), a 3rd Squadron was formed. Likewise, with the I-16s, three squadrons were initially formed.

These squadrons had Soviet pilots, although the 1st Squadron was completed with the Frenchman Darry and the Spaniard Andrés García Lacalle. Other aircraft that the Soviets also sent very discreetly to Spain was the modern twin-engine Tupolev SB-2 bomber, which was known as the *Katiuska* by the Republicans, while the Nationalists again, not knowing where it came from, confused it with the American Martin B-10 bomber, calling it the 'Martin bomber'. In the first shipments, 30 SB-2s arrived in Spain and were distributed in three squadrons that were assigned to Group 12 (with bases in the vicinity of Albacete). The arrival of the weapons (mainly aircraft and tanks) from the Soviet Union, and above all their high quality, surprised both sides in Spain.

The arrival of the Soviet materiel, as we have already mentioned, caught the Nationalists by surprise. They were surprised when several *Katiuskas* attacked the airfields in Córdoba, Granada, Seville, Cáceres, Salamanca and Talavera on 29 October with almost total impunity (the CR.32s did not have enough speed to reach them) or the I-15s strafed the Nationalist troops on the Toledo road (where ground troops with Soviet-made T-26 tanks also took part). The rapid advance of the Nationalist troops on all fronts was suddenly halted by the irruption of modern military equipment, which in the field of aviation was represented at first by the agile I-15s and the fast SB-2s, although other aircraft of great military value were soon to appear.

The first Soviet crew members to arrive in Spain numbered about 150 and were commanded by Lieutenant General Yakov Smuschkevich (alias General Douglas), an experienced officer of the VVS (*Voenno-Vozdushnye Sily* or Soviet Air Force).

In conjunction with the arrival of Soviet aircraft, and other weapons, and the manufacture of Soviet-patented I-15 aircraft in Spain, it was also decided to send groups of 200 pilots to the Soviet Union. This idea allowed the level of the Republican (Spanish) pilots to rise significantly, although it also led to complicated journeys across Europe.

The FARE was still enjoying the arrival of the powerful I-15s when the modern Polikarpov I-16 monoplanes began to arrive. These powerful planes came in boxes bearing their origin in Cyrillic (*Moskba*, which in Russian is Moscow), but in Spain they were called '*Mosca*' because of the similarity of the word and the small size of the plane to a fly. On the Nationalist side, when their presence was discovered, they were less affectionately referred to as 'Rata' (Rat). There were 62 of the first I-16s to arrive in Spain with their Soviet pilots, and after being assembled they were able to make their combat debut on 15 November, surprising the Nationalists who were fighting to conquer Madrid with their speed. The arrival of first the I-15s and then the I-16s largely prevented Madrid from being captured by General Varela's troops.

When the I-16 arrived in Spain, the Nationalist side was very surprised and even thought that they were American-made Curtiss aircraft.

When the Tupolev SB-2 appeared in Spanish skies, many mistook it for the American-made Martin bomber.

The I-16s were decisive in the Battle of Madrid when they joined the I-15s on 15 November 1936. The photograph was taken at El Carmolí.

The three types of Soviet aircraft that arrived in October after being assembled took part in the fighting over the city of Madrid, causing a great impression and damage to the enemy.

The first action by Soviet aircraft was by SB-2s on 28–29 October when they dropped their cargo of bombs on the airfields of Seville and Cáceres. Although CR.32s took off, they were unable to intercept them due to their slower speed.

The arrival of Soviet planes and pilots in the Madrid sector turned the course of events in the air, while on the ground the brigades of foreign volunteers fighting for the Republic managed to put a complete stop to the Nationalist advance.

Above Madrid, an intense battle was fought by both sides determined to take control of the skies.

On 4 November, the two squadrons of 'Chatos' entered combat for the first time, one in Madrid (commanded by Pyotr Pumpur and Pavel Rygachov). On the other hand, another one with a smaller number of aircraft was created in Vizcaya (these belonged to a shipment that arrived on the merchant ship *A. Andreev* on 1 November in Bilbao with 15 I-15s) which would quickly give the FARE initial air superiority in northern Spain, taking part in the failed Republican offensive against the Álava area when they failed in the attempt to capture Vitoria. The squadron was commanded by the Soviet Boris Marenchov and, unlike the rest of the I-15 squadrons, most of the pilots were Spanish and not Soviet. Against them the main fighters of the National Aviation (CR.32s and He 51s) had great difficulties in trying to take control of the skies from these unknown fighters. In fact, the He 51 was clearly inferior to the Soviet fighter while the CR.32 had similar characteristics.

The I-15 pilots flew up to four sorties during the busiest days in the skies over Madrid, claiming four enemy aircraft in just 10 minutes in their first mission on 4 November. On their second sortie of the day they managed to intercept six Ju 52s, of which they shot down one, to reach the figure of five enemy fighters and two bombers shot down by the end of the day. No I-15s were shot down, but two strayed and landed in Segovia (held by the Nationalist side) and the planes were captured and their origin discovered.

On 5 November there was another important clash over Leganés (Madrid) between nine CR.32s escorting three Ro.37s and 15 I-15s escorting several Potez 54 bombers. The CR.32s flew in three groups of three planes with Captain Maccagno in command. Maccagno was shot down in combat against the I-15s and was captured on the ground. In this engagement, García Morato shot down one I-15 and damaged a Potez 54, and Salas Larrazábal shot down one I-15 and damaged two others; the other Spanish pilot, Salvador, did not manage to shoot down any enemy aircraft. Regarding this combat on 5 November, the Nationalist pilot Salas Larrazábal noted in his logbook: '…our Fiats encountered about 15 "Curtiss" fighters. I took one by surprise and shot it down, the plane fell about 5 kilometres south-southeast of Barajas…'.

On 6 November five CR.32s (with Italian and Spanish pilots commanded by Captain Salas Larrazábal) engaged seven I-15s, claiming four of them as shot down (although only two were confirmed down); while the Soviets claimed the downing of a CR.32 (confirmed) and a Ju 52 (which was only damaged).

On 9 November García Morato claimed to have shot down a 'Curtiss fighter' as well as attacking eight SB-2s which he prevented from dropping their bombs. On the opposing side, Lieutenant Zakharov claimed to have shot down a German Arado aircraft (which turned out to be a Romeo Ro.37).

German pilot Hannes Trautloft describes in his diary on 10 November one of the encounters of his He 51s with SB-2s in the fighting around Madrid and the inability of the German fighter to reach them:

> Some Ju's and He 46s, escorted by us, intervene in the fighting and bombard the Reds' positions. Near Getafe we suddenly receive anti-aircraft artillery fire from our own batteries. While I'm still coughing up toads and snakes about it, I see that the flak is not aimed at us at all, but at three Red "Martin" bombers. One is hit full on, blown to pieces and it is chillingly beautiful to see the wreckage whizzing into the air. The other two Russian bomber planes equipped with a fixed machine gun attack our Ju's from behind. When we arrive they flee. Unfortunately they are too fast, it is impossible to catch them with our good old He 51s.

On 13 November five Ju 52s and three Ro.37s escorted by 14 CR.32s were attacked by 16 I-15s. The final result of this combat was that the Soviets claimed the downing of six aircraft (in exchange for two of their own aircraft shot down), while the Nationalist CR.32 claimed the downing of nine enemy aircraft (with damage to three I-15s and four SB-2s). On the same day there was another important clash in the skies over Madrid between CR.32s and He 51s against I-15s with a significant number of casualties on both sides. The CR.32s were based at Torrijos-Barciense airfield (Toledo) and the He 51s at Ávila. From Ávila (which three days earlier had been attacked by SB-2s that destroyed several He 51, Ju 52 and He 46 aircraft) nine He 51s departed to escort five Ju 52s and three Heinkel He 46s to attack the west bank of the Manzanares river (outside Madrid). The most intense moment of the engagement came when 12 I-15s and 12 I-16s (commanded by Lieutenant Pavel Rygachov and Captain Sergey Tarkhov respectively) launched themselves against the AN formation. The violent clash between the two formations resulted in the loss of two I-16s and five I-15s on the Republican side and only the loss of two He 51s on the German side, but with the concern that the I-16 fighters, according to *Leutnant* (Lieutenant) Wolf-Heinrich von Houwald, 'could play with us as they wished'.

Luis Sirvent's testimony (taken from the article by José Galán Ortega) about the appearance of the I-16s in the skies over Madrid, still dominated by the Nationalist side, reflects the boost to morale that their arrival represented:

> A dozen tiny blue fighters appeared on their underside, very fast, which fell like lightning on the Francoist trimotors, setting one on fire a few seconds after starting the fight […]. Only a few minutes had passed when the powerful formation of trimotors had transformed into a disbanded, disorderly fleeing from the pursuit of the monoplanes; which shot down, in flames, two more bombers […] The morale of the Madrilenians went through the roof with that first act of presence of the government aviation. At the end of the aerial combat, our fighters devoted a few minutes to their aerobatic display before the people of Madrid, before retiring to their base.

The AN had to increase the number of CR.32 squadrons to three in November, but on the Republican side the I-16s were clearly superior to the Italian-made aircraft (only superior in dive speed and manoeuvrability) and of course to the He 51s. In these fights in November pilots such as García Morato and Salas Larrazábal (in the AN) and García Lacalle (in the FARE) stood out, while the Ju 52s and Ro.37s continued to attack the airfields near Madrid (being forbidden to bomb the city).

On 15 November four I-16s engaged a grouping of CR.32s over Navalcarnero (Madrid), shooting down two of the Italian-built fighters. It was clear that air supremacy had changed sides with the arrival of the Soviet fighters.

On 16 November in an engagement between CR.32s escorting bombers and I-15s commanded by Rygachov, Rygachov was shot down by Brigadier Brunetto di Montegnacco, and parachuted out and lightly wounded. Command of the I-15 squadron, known as the 'Palancar Squadron', was taken over by Piotr Pumpur.

Soviet deliveries continued with two more types of aircraft, in this case attack aircraft. The first was the Polikarpov R-5 (of the R-5SSS model), of which 31 landed in the port of Cartagena from the merchant ship *Aldecoa* on 19 November. They were immediately sent to the base at Los Alcázares where they were assembled and manned by Soviets. These aircraft would enter combat shortly afterwards, on 2 December as part of Group 31 (under the command of Soviet Major Konstantin Gusev), replacing the Breguet XIX. The R-5 was similar to the Breguet XIX but slightly superior. The R-5s were based at the airfields of Villamayor, Quintanar and Santacruz in the fighting over Madrid, mainly targeting enemy airfields and positions. Subsequently, the FARE's attack aircraft would be complemented by the penultimate type of Soviet aircraft sent from the Soviet Union, the Polikarpov R-Z, which arrived in Spain in January 1937.

The last major battle during the Nationalist offensive for Madrid took place on 19 November when a formation of four SM.81s, 12 Ro.37s and 18 Ju 52s escorted by 16 CR.32s and nine He 51s was intercepted by more than 30 I-15 and I-16 fighters. During the massive clash in the skies over Madrid, the Republicans shot down two fighters and one Ju 52 and damaged two Ju 52s; while the Nationalists claimed the downing of seven Soviet fighters (although the Republican side only acknowledged the downing of one I-15 and one I-16). Also three SM.81s were damaged at their base by an attack by R-5s commanded by Major Goosev himself on the airfield of Velada (Talavera de la Reina in Toledo).

The Polikarpov R-5 SSS 'Rasante' arrived in Spain on 19 November 1936. On 2 December the 31 aircraft received took part in the attack on the airfield of Velada (in Talavera) destroying several Italian SM.81s. This picture also shows a pair of I-16s.

Interesting photograph of a He 51 after a crash during landing. It allows us to see the Nationalist insignia on the upper wing.

The indisputable fact is that by the end of November the initiative in the air was with the Republican side, whose modern fighter planes prevented Nationalist daylight bombing; and of course, Madrid resisted the offensive. Despite the Nationalists' failure to capture Madrid, on 18 November Germany and Italy recognised Francisco Franco as head of the Spanish state, indicating their willingness to continue supporting the Nationalists.

Although the battle for Madrid was almost over, at the end of November the Republic's air force bombed the Gamonal (Toledo) airfield, damaging three aircraft. On 2 December, 18 Polikarpov R-5s attacked the airfield at Veladas (Toledo) destroying an SM.81 and leaving two SM.81s damaged (losing one R-5). On 4 December the R-5s damaged four Ju 52s in another attack, while on 7 December they attacked the Torrijos (Toledo) airfield. That same day the *Katiuskas* attacked the airfields of Veladas and Tablada (Seville), as well as Salamanca, Granada, Córdoba and Burgos.

The heavy attrition on both sides in the air and on the ground during the offensive for Madrid meant that at the beginning of December military operations were scaled down, with some of the fighters on both sides being transferred to other fronts such as the Aragón front.

The Condor Legion

Before moving on to the fighting in Aragón, it should be remembered that the arrival in Spain of huge quantities of war materiel from the Soviet Union set off alarm bells in Berlin due to the great technical difference between German aircraft in Spain and those of the Soviets. So, in response to the Soviet expeditionary force, on 7 November the German government decided to form the Condor Legion. Both personnel and war materiel began to be assembled in Baltic ports in complete secrecy. In fact, its air component was codenamed *Eiserne rationen* (Iron Rations), later changed to *Eiserne Legion* and finally renamed the Condor Legion (*Legion Condor* in German).

This all-German unit was composed of ground troops and about 100 aircraft, totalling some 4,500 volunteers under the command of Major General Hugo Otto Sperrle. It arrived in Spain in November 1936 and was organised a shown in Table 5.

Table 5: Organisation of the Condor Legion, November 1936

Senior commander: *Generalmajor* Sperrle	
Führungsstab S/88	General Staff
Jagdgruppe J/88	Fighter group with 4 squadrons of Heinkel He 51 (48 aircraft)
Kampfgruppe K/88	Bomber group with 4 squadrons of Junkers Ju 52 (48 aircraft)
Aufklärungsstaffel A/88	Reconnaissance group with 4 squadrons: 3 long-range reconnaissance squadrons equipped with Heinkel He 70 (18 aircraft) 1 short-range reconnaissance squadron equipped with Heinkel He 45 (6 aircraft)
Gemischte Aufklärungs- und Bombenstaffel See AS/88	Naval reconnaissance group consisting of 2 squadrons: 1 squadron equipped with Heinkel He 59 (10 aircraft) 1 squadron equipped with Heinkel He 60 (6 aircraft)
Luftnachrichten-Abteilung Ln/88	Signals battalion consisting of four companies
Flak Abteilung F/88	Anti-aircraft battalion equipped with six batteries. 2 batteries equipped with 20 mm FlaK-30 (10 pieces) 4 batteries equipped with 88 mm FlaK-18 (20 pieces)

Luftzeuggruppe und Luftpark P/88	Two *Luftwaffe* maintenance companies
Munitions-Anstalt MA/88	Ammunition depot
Sanitäts-Abteilung San/88	Medical battalion
Lazarett Laz/88	Field hospital
Wetterstelle W/88	Meteorological unit

The German unit, as can be seen, had its own ground crew, in addition to its air forces. The men of the Condor Legion acted under their own command and had a great deal of autonomy in their operation, although operations would be carried out in coordination with the Nationalist army. Their main targets would be the ports through which Soviet materiel arrived by ship, and Spanish soldiers were requested to provide ground protection for their air bases.

The first contingent of men for the Condor Legion were 697 volunteers who embarked in Stettin on 7 November on the ship *Fulda*, arriving in Seville on the 16th. On the 18th the ships *St. Louis* and *Berlin* arrived in Cádiz from Swinemünde carrying the first He 51s for the German unit, disguised as agricultural machinery. On the same day, 31 Ju 52s flew from Greifswald to Seville.

The first two Heinkel He 70Fs to arrive in Spain arrived just before the formation of the Condor Legion and were used for strategic raids over enemy territory on reconnaissance missions over enemy airfields or communications hubs. Due to their high speed, they were given the name *Rayo* (Lightning) as they were practically unreachable by enemy aircraft.

As for the fighter unit, the J/88, the first three squadrons (1.J/88, 2.J/88 and 3.J/88) composed of He 51s, these aircraft were landed at Cádiz and assembled at Tablada (Seville) where they arrived on 18 November. They were placed under the command of captains (*Hauptmann*) Werner Palm, Siegfried Lehmann and Jürgen Roth. Their particular squadrons were intended for ground attack and not as fighters. With the pilots already in Spain flying He 51s, a fourth squadron (4.J/88) was formed under the command of Captain Herwig Knüppel. The nicknames of the four squadrons (*staffeln* in German) were: *Marabou*, *Zylinder Hut*, *Mickey Mouse* and *Wilder Jäger* (later *Pik As*) respectively.

At the end of November Wolfram Freiherr von Richthofen arrived in Seville to take charge of a small unit within the Condor Legion for the combat testing of prototype aircraft, which was named *Versuchsgruppe 88*, *Versuchssrtaffel 88*, or *Versuchsjagdgruppe 88* (VJ/88). This unit was organised during December 1936 and had a small number of the novel Messerschmitt Bf 109 and a prototype of the Heinkel He 112. Both aircraft, especially the former, would in the following years demonstrate the German victory in fighter production in the second half of the 1930s.

The Condor Legion, which immediately went into action with a bombing raid on the evening of 25 November, at night, on the Cartagena naval base carried out by the three squadrons of Junkers Ju 52 under the command of Group Commander Fuchs.

Despite the significant German effort in bringing such important war materiel to Spain, it is important to note that both the fighter and bomber planes of the Condor Legion were of inferior quality and performance to those of the Soviets on the Republican side when they arrived in Spain.

A Heinkel He 60 from the National Aviation. The Germans brought six of these aircraft in November 1936 to Spain and in April 1937 handed them over to the National Aviation.

One of the Heinkel He 51s belonging to the 2.J/88 *Zylinderhut* (Top Hat) as can be seen from the emblem on the fuselage.

A joint parade of Spanish and German troops at a Nationalist airfield. One of the Ju 52s can be seen in the background.

Two Condor Legion pilots protect themselves from the rain in front of one of their He 51s.

Several Condor Legion pilots walking on an airfield pass in front of a Bf 109.

The Ju 52 was inferior in speed to the SB-2 and the He 51 was inferior to the I-15 and I-16. This would lead to the He 51 finishing the SCW as an attack aircraft, where it performed well.

On 5 December Captain Hubertus Methart von Bernegg, as commander of J/88, requested the transfer of two pilots from the unit to Seville to test the first Bf 109s to arrive in Spain. The pilots were Lieutenant Hannes Trauloft and *Unteroffizier* Erwin Kley, and they began testing immediately. The first flight was made by Trauloft on 14 December and a few days later Kley had an accident with one of the Bf 109s. When the Bf 109s began to arrive in adequate numbers in Spain, they became the best of the SCW fighters, again giving the Nationalists the upper hand in the air.

In December, after being landed in Cádiz, the prototype of an aircraft that would become world famous during the following years arrived at the Condor Legion: the Junkers Ju 87 V4. This dive bomber aircraft was incorporated into the VJ/88 (as happened with the first two Hs 123s that arrived in Spain). The aircraft was based at Tablada airfield and flew its first combat mission on 31 December over the Córdoba area. As it was considered a 'secret' aircraft, all its actions remained hidden. After a series of test flights during the month of January, it was probably disassembled and returned to Germany with a large amount of information that would be used by Junkers to improve the prototype of the aircraft.

Another very interesting aspect of the German unit was the creation of regular communication with the Reich by means of a Junkers Ju 52 that brought mail directly from Germany, although it also allowed the 'legionnaires' to be sent various products such as beer and butter. In this respect, even bottled mineral water was supplied by ship from the Reich to their home ports in Spain.

Battles in Álava and Teruel

The Republican offensive towards Vitoria began on 30 November. On that date, six Nationalist planes based in Burgos (two Fokkers, a DH Dragon and three Breguet XIXs) discovered 40 trucks near Villarreal in Álava, which they attacked and succeeded in blocking the road. In response to the attack, the Nationalists sent planes to Lacua (Vitoria).

On 2 December, the nine I-15s from Bilbao together with the Breguet XIXs, Vildebeests, Monospars and others, carried out three missions in the morning, bombing Vitoria during the third. The situation at Villarreal became critical for the Nationalists, but it held out despite further Republican attacks between the 12th and 14th.

On the 12th the Bilbao planes damaged a DH Dragon at Lacua and lost a Monospar. In reply, on the 13th nine German He 51s together with the Spanish Breguets and Fokkers, carried out continuous war operations. So, one Fokker had to land 5km from Lacua and the other went to the Crew School. On the 28th the DH Dragon was again strafed and was out of service for some time. After this, the Nationalists were left with only the Breguet XIXs and the He 51s.

Meanwhile in Aragón, and more specifically in Teruel, there was a Republican offensive with troops from Valencia. As air support, a squadron of I-15 fighters, the Potez 54s (piloted by both foreigners and Spaniards) and a few Breguet XIX and Nieuport Ni52 fighters were concentrated at the Manises and La Señera airfields. Against them, the National Aviation placed six He 51s at Caudé, very close to the front line.

As both aircraft were very active, they suffered several casualties in their combat actions. On 26 December, one of the He 51s crashed and a Potez 54 crashed on take-off, a second Potez was hit by enemy fire and a third crashed at Valdelinares on the flight back to base. A Ni52 crashed into a Latécoère-28, both loaded with fuel, and both aircraft quickly caught fire. Of the five He 51s in service, one was shot down, and the other four strafed by I-15s on 29 December at Caudé airfield, which meant that all the He 51s had to be sent to Seville by train for repairs.

Changes in Nationalist and Italian Aviation

With the arrival of a large amount of modern military equipment from the Soviet Union, the Italian contingent had to be adapted to the new situation. So, on 28 December the Aviation of the Tercio (in which the Italians were incorporated as legionnaires in the service

Messerschmitt Bf 109 V4 (6-1). This was one of three prototypes of this fighter that arrived by ship in Cadiz in December 1936. It was flown by the famous German ace Otto Hans "Hannes" Trautloft. Of particular note is the green heart emblem, placed by its pilot, which became a few years later the emblem of the Luftwaffe Jagdgeschwader 54 during the Second World War. (Artwork by Jean-Marie Guillou)

Boeing Model 281. This demonstrator aircraft was requisitioned by the Spanish government and incorporated into its air force. Its pilot in October 1936 was Ramón Puparelli. It was the only aircraft of its type to fly during the SCW. (Artwork by Jean-Marie Guillou)

Nieuport-Delage Ni52C.1 (3-30) of the 23rd Group as can be seen by its quatrefoil emblem. This aircraft based at Sariñena was flown by Jesús García Herguido between August and October 1936. (Artwork by Jean-Marie Guillou)

Nieuport-Delage Ni52C.1 (3-8) bearing the No. 12 Group emblem. Although by this time the Group had been disbanded, having been deployed from its Getafe base to the Andújar airfield by the government side. (Artwork by Jean-Marie Guillou)

Fiat CR.32 (NC 103), Talavera de la Reina (Toledo), September 1936. This was one of the first Italian-made fighters to fight for the rebel side in Spain. This particular one belonged to the 2nd Aviation Fighter Squadron of the Tercio and was flown by the Spanish ace Ángel Salas Larrazábal. (Artwork by Jean-Marie Guillou)

Fiat CR.32. Talavera de la Reina (Toledo), September-October 1936. This aircraft was flown by Sottotenente Giuseppe Cenni of the 1st Aviation Fighter Squadron of the Tercio. The inscription "MONICO! PRESENTE" in homage to Lieutenant Ernesto Monico, shot down on 31 August 1936 and subsequently shot by government forces. (Artwork by Jean-Marie Guillou)

One of the Junkers Ju 52 3m (the *Maria Magdalena*) of the 3rd Ju 52 squadron created in August 1936. This 3rd squadron (3-E-22) would later become the 4th squadron (4-E-22). On the front is the inscription "TRECHUELO" in homage to Francisco Díaz Trechuelo, one of the commanders of the Ju 52 squadrons of the Nationalist side who died at the beginning of the war when he was hit by a rifle shot while flying over Badajoz on a mission. (Artwork by Jean-Marie Guillou)

Potez 540 (n/f 4219). This French-built aircraft shows a large "F" on its tail and the inscription on the starboard side "¡AQUÍ TE ESPERO! This aircraft commanded by Joaquín Mellado Pascual (head of the Potez Group) took part in the unsuccessful attack on the cruiser *Canarias* in Ferrol. Only two days later, on 25 September 1936, it was shot down. (Artwork by Jean-Marie Guillou)

The Polikarpov I-15 was, together with the I-16, the basis of the fighters of the Republic. It was known as the *Chato* by the Republicans and *Curtiss* by the Nationalists. Some of the I-15s were purchased from the Soviet Union and others were built under licence in Spain. The Spanish-built ones bore the code CA on the fuselage, while the Soviet ones had the code CC, like the one in the picture. (Artwork by Jean-Marie Guillou)

One of the first two Henschel Hs 123s to arrive in Spain (for the Nationalist side) in the second week of September 1936. Its call sign was 501 and it bore the inscription "ANGELITO 1". It was precisely this aircraft that would be known in Spain as Angelito. (Artwork by Jean-Marie Guillou)

The Hawker Fury was the aircraft selected by the Spanish Republic to be the fighter of its air force before the start of the SCW, replacing the Nieuport-Delage Ni52C.1. At the start of the war in Spain there were only three examples, which also had no armament. One Fury was captured by the rebels, another was shot down on the Madrid front in November 1936 and the third Fury remained in service until 1938 when it was decommissioned due to lack of spare parts. The aircraft in the picture, a Hawker Fury MK. IIC (4-2) shows the Republican flag on the tail and the red band on the fuselage, as well as the tricolour cockade on the wings, typical of the Republican side. (Artwork by Jean-Marie Guillou)

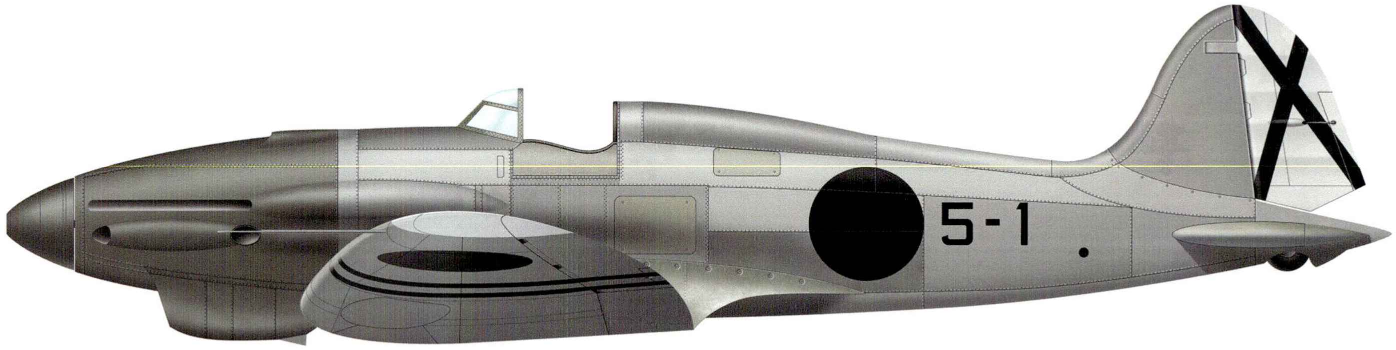

Heinkel He-112 V3 (WNr 1292). This prototype aircraft was used as a gunship fighter (a concept later developed with the Bf 110 Zerstörer in the Luftwaffe). The aircraft, known as the *Kanonenvogel* (gunship bird) was flown by *Oberleutnant* Günther "Fips" Radusch, and began flying on 22 December 1936. (Artwork by Jean-Marie Guillou)

Polikarpov I-16 Type 10 (CM-177) belonging to the 4th Squadron. This aircraft is notable for its Popeye emblem, as well as the red stripe on the fuselage and the tricolour flag on the tail. The arrival of this model in the SCW was a great concern for the rebel side. It was known as *Mosca* (fly) to the government side and *Rata* (rat) to the rebels. (Artwork by Jean-Marie Guillou)

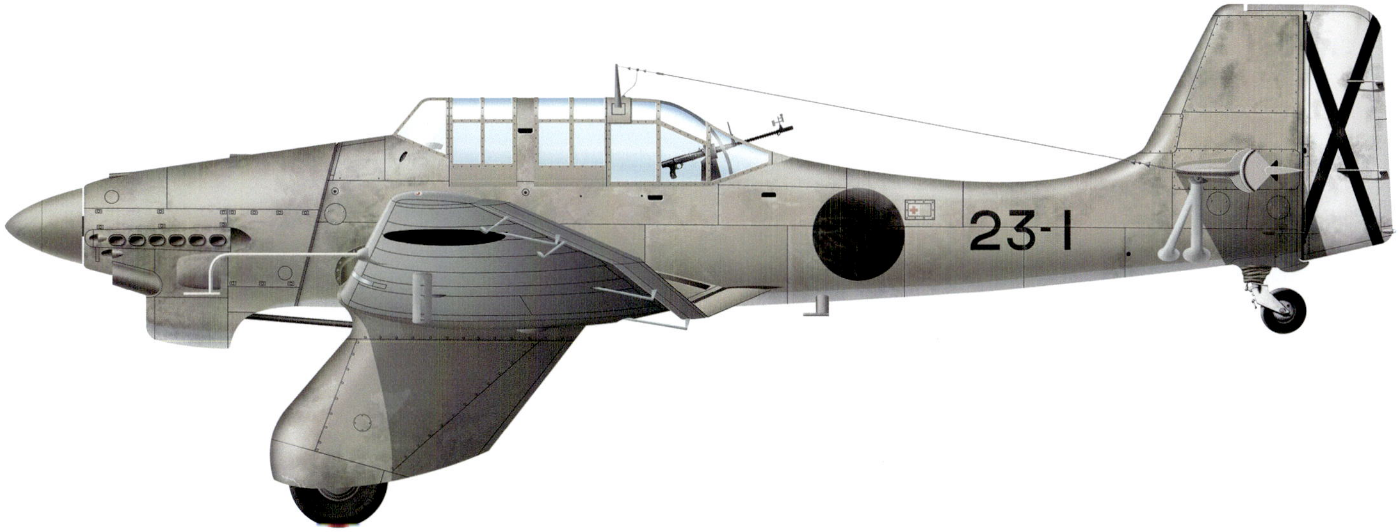

Junkers Ju 87 V4 (WNr 4924) 23-1. This prototype of the famous German attack aircraft arrived in Spain in December 1936 and was tested in combat situations from its base at Tablada (Seville). (Artwork by Jean-Marie Guillou)

Messerschmitt Bf 109B (6 34) belonging to 1.J/88. This aircraft was flown by *Oberleutnant* Erich Woitke. The arrival of the Bf 109s in the skies over Spain was an important boost for the aviation of the rebel side. Note the four victory marks on the tail and the small white "x" on the black insignia of the fuselage. (Artwork by Jean-Marie Guillou)

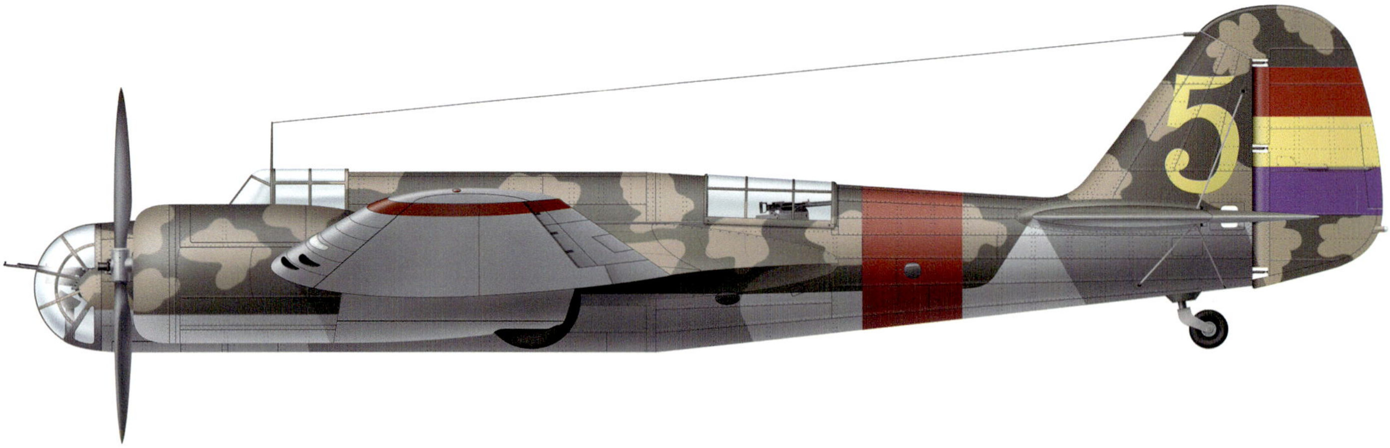

Tupolev SB-2M (5) belonging to *Grupo 12*. This aircraft features the Republican tricolour flag on its tail. The *Katiuska* (as these aircraft were known) of the 12th Group were very active in attacks against Nationalist emplacements, causing them a great deal of wear and tear. In the first 15 days of operations, eight Tupolev SB-2Ms were lost. (Artwork by Jean-Marie Guillou)

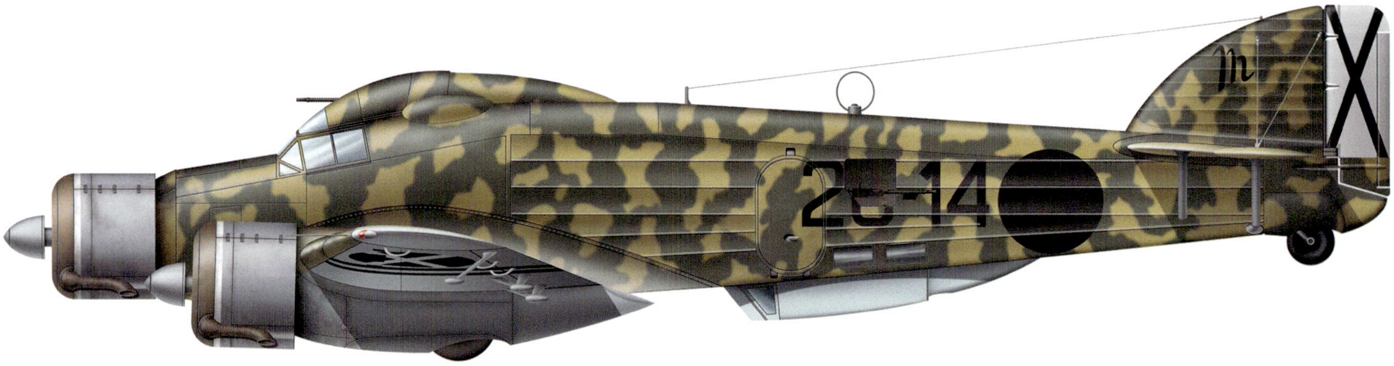

Savoia Marchetti SM 79. The Italian-made SM.79 light bombers of the Italian Aviazione Legionaria were, together with the SB-2s of the Republican side, the best bombers of the SCW. Note the "M" on the tail, for Mussolini. (Artwork by Jean-Marie Guillou)

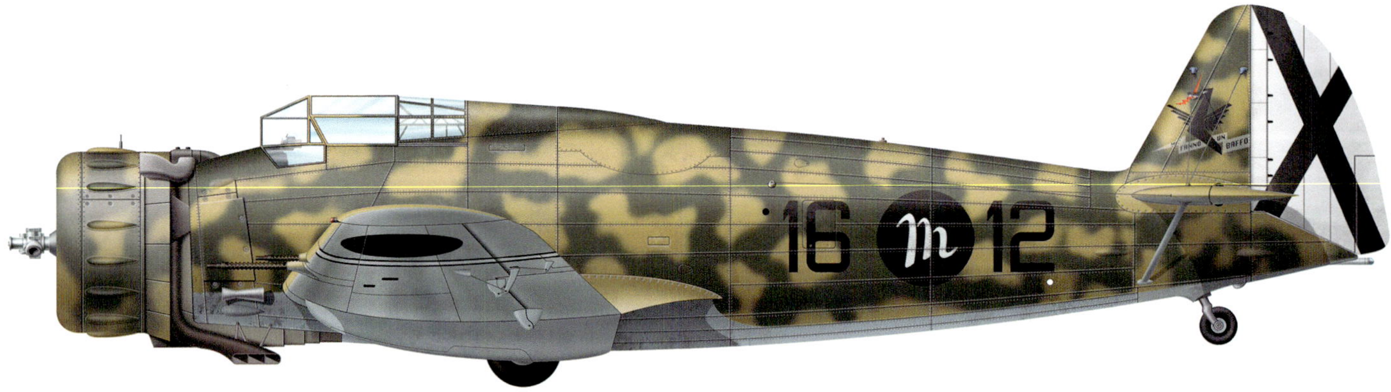

Breda Ba.65 of the *Aviazione Legionaria*. These Italian-made assault aircraft belonged to the 65th Assault Squadron (*65 Squadriglia d'Assalto de la Aviazione Legionaria*) and were used with little success in the SCW. (Artwork by Jean-Marie Guillou)

Heinkel He 111B-1 (25 7) of the Condor Legion, summer 1937. This aircraft has the emblem known as "Glitzer Mary's 4 Grad" and on the front it has the inscription "PEDRO". This German bomber was known as the *Pedro* in Spain. (Artwork by Jean-Marie Guillou)

Heinkel He 59B-2 belonging to the *Aufklärungsstaffel See 88*, as can be seen by its Ace of Spades emblem. These aircraft from their base in Pollensa would be a very active enemy for the Republic of Spain's maritime communications in the Mediterranean. (Artwork by Jean-Marie Guillou)

Nieuport-Delage Ni52C.1 captured by the rebel forces at the beginning of the SCW. We can see that the aircraft had belonged to the 12th Group. The aircraft has the St. Andrew's Cross on the tail, the black circle on the wing and dark paint markings to camouflage it better. (Artwork by Jean-Marie Guillou)

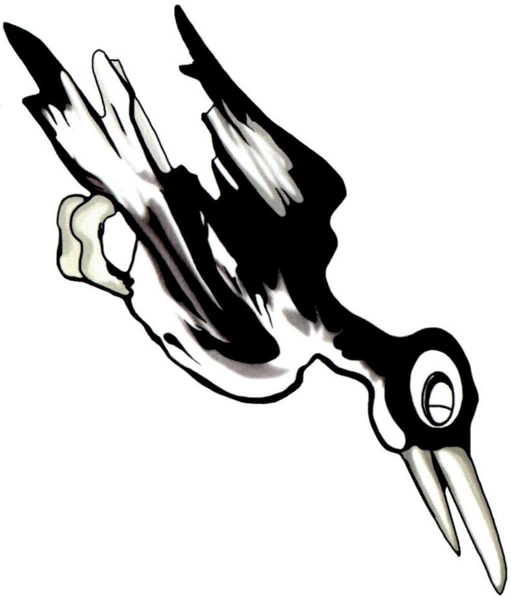

The emblem of 1.J/88, was a Hababuk, a bird similar to a crow, with a white beak. There were several variants of this emblem. (Artwork by Jean-Marie Guillou)

A black disc with the Cross of St. Andrew painted in white was used as an emblem painted on the Bf 109s of 1.J/88 from April 1937 to September 1938. (Artwork by Jean-Marie Guillou)

Another emblem used by 1.J/88 was the *Holzauge* (wooden eye) which meant 'look out'. The 'Wood Eye' – the English equivalent being 'Dead Eye' – represented an expert marksman. The image is of a clown inside a white circle pointing at its eye, while at the same time it glances at the sky. (Artwork by Jean-Marie Guillou)

Above: The Bf 109 V4 belonging to *Oberleutnant* Hannes Trauloft, recognisable by its green heart emblem. This was one of the first three Bf 109s to arrive in Spain.

Right: Several Breguet XIXs from the rebel side at an airfield in northern Spain preparing for the next flight.

Below: An I-15 preparing for take-off. These aircraft were initially flown by Soviets and were later flown by Spaniards.

of Spain) was disbanded to create the *Aviazione Legionaria* or AL (Legionary Aviation). The role of the Tercio Aviation during those almost six months was important as they shot down 131 enemy aircraft, although other sources put it at just over 80 (plus 14 probable), of which 16 were by Spanish pilots flying their CR.32s.

A squadron of He 51s are prepared for take-off in a few minutes.

This new air corps retained the personnel and aircraft of the Tercio Aviation, but it would now be an Italian unit. As was the case with the Tercio Aviation, there were a number of Spanish soldiers and pilots in this unit. With the six squadrons of CR.32s, the *XVI Gruppo 'La Cucaracha'* (formed by *Squadriglie 24ª, 25ª* and *26ª*) was created, and in April 1937 the *XXIII Gruppo 'Asso di Bastoni'*. Somewhat later (mid-1937) a third unit was created, the *VI Gruppo 'Leónello'* (which became better known as *'Gamba di Ferro'* from the spring of 1938).

In addition to the AL, there remained in Spain, albeit autonomously, another Italian unit in the Balearic Islands (although it also had several seaplanes with Spanish crews) known as *Aviazione Legionaria delle Baleari*. Specifically, the CR.32s equipped the *X Gruppo Caccia 'Baleari'* (formed by the 101st and 102nd Squadrons) and the *Squadriglia Autonoma Mitragliamento* (independent fighting and strafing squadron) *'Frecce'* (Arrows) composed of 12 CR.32bis initially armed with four guns.

For its part, the National Aviation was increasing the number of aircraft it had with each passing day. Even so, these corresponded to a mixture of many different outdated models, to which must be added some more modern aircraft from Germany and Italy, including the Ju 52, He 51 and CR.32. As has been shown, the most capable Spanish pilots flew in the *Aviación del Tercio* under Italian command. Sooner or later these Spanish pilots had to be incorporated into the AN and it was on 22 December when García Morato flew to Tablada to start organising a modern fighter unit (with CR.32s) independent of the Italians. The idea was well received and at the end of December five CR.32s were received in Seville to form the nucleus of that unit, the so-called Blue Patrol.

A very significant event was the arrival in Spain (specifically in the port of Cádiz) in December 1936 of the first three Bf 109 aircraft. These were three prototypes (the Bf 109V3, Bf 109V4 and Bf 109V6). Alongside them was another prototype fighter, the Heinkel He 112V3 (another fighter, but armed with a cannon that gave it great punch). Above all, the Bf 109 was to become one of the most important fighters in the world and the one produced in greatest numbers in the following years of the Second World War.

An SM.81 of the National Aviation escorted by CR.32 fighters of the *XVI Gruppo Cucaracha*.

Two Breda Ba.65 of the Aviazione Legionaria ready for their next mission. These assault aircraft belonged to the 65th Assault Squadron. (*65 Squadriglia d'Assalto de la Aviazione Legionaria*)

The prototype of the new German He 112V3 fighter already in Spain for intensive combat testing.

Nice photograph of a Fiat CR.32 with the insignia of the rebel side. Although they were not particularly outstanding in combat when they arrived in the SCW, little by little the increased skill of the pilots made them the real spearhead of the National Aviation.

Front line in the SCW in November 1936. Brown (Nationalist band), Pink (Republican band). (Public domain by POR TYK)

3

1937

Aviation at the Beginning of 1937

At the beginning of 1937 the air war situation in Spain was a small international conflict, with five air forces flying simultaneously. On the Nationalist side were the *Aviación Nacional, Legión Cóndor* and *Aviazione Legionaria*; while on the Republican side were the FARE and the Soviet air force which, although under Spanish command, actually acted with a great deal of freedom.

With the arrival of new, modern aircraft on both sides, the more obsolete models began to be used on secondary fronts or in rearguard duties. On the Republican side, for example, non-Russian materiel was used for rearguard, night or coastal defence duties.

In the FARE, there were various restructurings and the creation of new units thanks to the arrival of aircraft from the Soviet Union. Initially, the Russian materiel formed the 12th Group, from which the R-5 and R-Z cooperation aircraft were later separated to form the 15th and 20th Groups. As for the fighters, there was the Kolesnikov Squadron (the original Group) and from January, four I-15 squadrons in the Centre-South: the Russians under Osadchii and Zotsenko and the Spaniards under García Lacalle and Alonso Santamaría (both captains from January and February of 1937, respectively). As a curiosity, the 1st Squadron of I-15 *Chatos* was known as the *Escuadrilla Palancar* (because it was initially commanded by Pavel Richagov known in Spain as Pablo Palancar) or *Escuadrilla Lacalle* as it was commanded by Andrés García Lacalle. The 2nd I-15 Squadron was known as *The Penguins*, in reference to the emblem they carried on their aircraft: a penguin in the Antarctic.

Another Soviet aircraft that arrived in Spain was the Polikarpov R-Z, whose first batch of 31 aircraft arrived in Spain in January 1937 and the second batch (also 31 aircraft) on the ship *Aldecoa* on 14 February 1937. After the arrival of these planes, known as *Natachas*, Spanish crews were trained (with Soviet instructors) at the El Carmolí base. Once the planes and men had been prepared, the R-Zs were assigned to Group 20, made up of three squadrons under the command of Spanish commander Abelardo Moreno.

Two other arrivals in Spain of R-Z took place on 1 and 21 May 1937 on the ships *Cabo Santo Tomé* and *Sac2* respectively, with

In February 1937, the first 31 *Natacha* aircraft were received, replacing the Vildebeest and R-5s in naval aviation duties.

Fiat CR.32 captured by the Republicans and used for coastal defence. These aircraft were also used for training purposes.

which Group 30 would be formed with three squadrons.

The Legionary Aviation, which provided Italian support, began 1937 with two groups of two squadrons (SM.81 and Ro.37) and another of five squadrons of CR.32s (one of them in formation) on the Peninsula, which was soon to be split up. In Mallorca, the *Gruppo Autonomo Baleari* had an SM.81 squadron and the Fiat and Macchi M.41 patrols.

An Italian SM.81 waiting at its airfield for a new mission against the enemy.

During the first months of the year, the Condor Legion began to receive modern pre-series aircraft in order to reverse the inferiority of its aircraft in Spain compared to those of Soviet manufacture. Thus, 14 Bf 109 V and A, three He 111 B, three Do 17 E-1 and three Ju 86D-1 were sent to Spain. Specifically, on 20 February 1937, the *Versuchsbomberstaffel/88* (VB/88) was formed at Tablada airfield with three squadrons made up of three aircraft (one with He 111B, another with Do 17E and another with the Ju 86D) which would be responsible for testing in combat the capabilities of the three types of modern bombers that Germany had designed. On the same day, 20 February, three He 111s, a Do 17 and three Ju 86s bombed the Linares (Jaén) railway station. The Do 17E would later be used not only as a bomber but also as a reconnaissance aircraft thanks to its high speed. It was followed by the Do 17 F-1 reconnaissance version, sent to Spain in April 1937 to replace the He 70 Fs delivered to the Nationalists.

For example, the Bf 109s, which began to arrive in February, were not operational until April (for the Biscay campaign). The arrival of these still experimental aircraft would lead to their gradual incorporation into the Condor Legion (it was in March when the He 51s were replaced by the Bf 109s in 2.J/88) The same happened with the He 111s, whose arrival meant that in K/88 each of the four squadrons had two patrols of He 111s and one of Ju 52s.

The only He 112V3 on test in Spain was transferred to the 2.J/88 in March 1937, based in Toledo at the time. This aircraft would be lost after a landing accident on 19 July 1937 at Escalona airfield. During its brief career, the He 112V3 was used in the battle of

An IMAM Ro.37bis reconnaissance aircraft of the *Aviazione Legionaria* during the SCW. (Public domain)

A pair of Fiat CR.32s of the *X Gruppo Baleari* flying over Mallorca in 1937. Public domain.

Considered to be one of the SCW's slimmest aircraft, the Do 17 in this photograph shows why it was nicknamed the 'flying pencil'.

A formation of Do 17s in flight. These aircraft were used for reconnaissance and bombing duties.

Above: Nice photograph showing the upper part of an He 70 with the typical insignia of the Nationalist side.

Left: A He 111E-1 of the K/88 during one of its bombing missions.

A Ju 87 A as can be recognised by its bulky 'legs'.

Brunete, where it destroyed three enemy armoured vehicles (such was the main use of the aircraft due to its powerful cannon).

Also, in January, on the 15th, three Ju 87As arrived in Spain and formed a *Stuka Kette* based in Calamocha (Teruel) where it coincided with the J/88 (at administrative level the Ju 87 unit was called 5.J/88).

As a curiosity, the Condor Legion, Russian and Italian fighter squadrons had 12 aircraft, but the Italian reconnaissance and bombing squadrons had only six. The Spanish fighter squadrons on the Nationalist side rarely had more than six or seven aircraft aircraft, and the bombing squadrons had only three.

The situation on the front lines continued with the rebel side advancing progressively in the north, but being held back by the Republican side, which was strong in the centre and southeast of the country.

Table 6: Deployment of the AN in mid-February 1937

Southern Sector	
In Tablada and nearby	
Group SM.81	13 SM.81
3rd Fiat Squadron	19 CR.32
Group 3-G-10	6 Br. XIX
García Morato Fiat Patrol	3 CR.32
In Armilla and La Roda	
4th and 5th Fiat Squadrons	22 CR.32
Group 4-G-12	6 Br. XIX
1st Romeo Squadron	12 Ro.37
	Total 76 aircraft
Central Sector	
In Torrijos	
1st and 2nd Fiat Squadron	23 CR.32
In Ávila, Escalona, V. Del Prado and Almorox	
Group J/88	31 He 51, 1 Bf 109, 1 He 112
In Veladas	
3 Spanish Ju 52 groups	18 Ju 52, 1 DH.89
In Talavera	
2nd Romeo Squadron	6 Ro.37
	TOTAL 76 aircraft

Table 7: FARE deployment in mid-February 1937 in the South and Central sectors

Fighters	**Base**	**Aircraft**
Kolesnikov Squadron	Guadalajara and Alcalá	22 I-16
Zotsenko Squadron	Alcázar	16 I-15
Osadchii Squadron	Almeria	23 I-15
Lacalle Squadron	Guadalajara	17 I-15
Alonso Squadron	San Javier	17 I-15
Total		95
Bombers		
2nd Squadron Group 15 (2/15)	Quintanar	12 R-5
2nd Squadron Group 20 (2/20)	Madridejos	12 R-Z
Group 12	Sisante and San Clemente	24 SB-2
Total		48

Possibly (although not fully confirmed) in February 1937 a new shipment of Polikarpov R-5 of the R-5Sht (Shturmovik) model arrived in Spain, specially prepared for ground attack not only with bombs but also with eight PV-1 machine guns.

First Air Combats in 1937

Italian aircraft had increased by 60 CR.32s between November 1936 and January 1937 due to the increased activity of Soviet-made aircraft. The German He 51 fighter was beginning to show its weaknesses as it failed to achieve air superiority and suffered heavy losses (up to 20 percent during January 1937). *Oberleutnant* Harro Harder's view of German inferiority in aircraft compared to Soviet-made aircraft is clear in his words:

> We were convinced that it was madness to continue sending He 51s on escort missions over Madrid. The "Ratas" were playing cat and mouse with us, and even the "Martin" bombers were at least 50km/h faster than our fighters. Pilot morale was excellent, but all the courage in the world was useless in the face of such technical inferiority.

In mid-January, *Hauptmann* Merhart, commander of *Jagdgruppe J/88*, wrote a report to *Generalmajor* Sperrle protesting the technical shortcomings of the He 51, which eventually led to the He 51s switching to mainly ground attack missions from their bases in Vitoria, León, Escalona and Ávila.

On the Republican side, between December 1936 and January 1937, 30 1-15s arrived in Spain from the Soviet Union, with which they were able to organise up to four squadrons of 10–12 aircraft each.

On 3 January, Captain García Morato faced several SB-2s, recounting:

> After spending several days studying the attacks on Córdoba I had managed to find out when and where the bombers usually appeared, at what altitude they were and the direction from which they tended to approach. Taking advantage of this information, I began to fly a permanent patrol at an altitude of 5,000 metres over the city. One morning, while flying over Córdoba, I noticed two planes heading towards the city at high speed. Heading towards them as fast as I could I immediately identified the contacts as the two twin-engine bombers that had been regularly attacking Córdoba. I opened fire and hit one of the engines of the first aircraft. It soon caught fire, leaving a trail of black smoke behind it. The damaged bomber turned, heading back the way it had come, and I followed it, expecting to see it crash (piloted by the Spaniard Ananías Sanjuán Alonso, the only survivor of the shootdown). I also saw the second bomber turn back towards home. The damaged bomber crashed about 60km from Córdoba, not far from the communist airport of Andújar. It was engulfed in flames. On the way back, my fighter was attacked by the second bomber. The twin-engine had somehow come within 300m and was firing at me with its two machine guns. This was a dangerous moment for me, as I was more than 30km from home territory. I had never thought that a bomber crew would dare to attack me. However, I kept my cool, turned sharply away, turned and fired at the enemy. As luck would have it, my bullets hit the plane in some vital spot and within seconds it went down (piloted by Bulgarian Nikolay Batov), crashing to the ground and exploding barely two kilometres from my first victim. I received hundreds of congratulations, the population was very happy.

On 4 January 20 He 51s of J/88 still acting as fighters during the escort of nine Ju 52s over Bilbao had an encounter with a group of eight I-15s. *Oberleutnant* Harder recounted:

> I hear machine guns behind. A "Red" comes at me sharply from above, I see its radial engine like a giant eye, I turn my plane and the "Red" is already being chased by two of our fighters. Far below, over the valley, I see a 1-15 circling. Using my superior speed, I know I can block it. I get behind him, fire, he turns, I cut him off, another turn, the smoke from my tracer shells disappears in his machine. Now he comes up, black, with a red band in front of his tail, spins on his back and sinks almost vertically into the ground. I pull myself together, the tension of the duel has made me lose contact with everything else. I see a He 51 nearby. Exhausted, I take to the air and fly to Vitoria where I celebrate my victory by making a barrel roll at low altitude over the airfield.

In this clash, three I-15s were claimed shot down by the Germans while two Ju 52s and two He 51s were lost in return, although it is difficult to know how many planes from either side were actually shot down.

The He 51 was converted during the SCW from a fighter to a ground attack aircraft due to the arrival of the powerful Soviet I-15s and I-16s.

Nice picture of a Ju 52 at Tablada airfield in Seville.

Another interesting account is given by Hannes Trautloft, in which he describes how the camaraderie between pilots of opposing sides was sometimes maintained:

> Over Bilbao the Reds shot down a Ju 52 for us. In the same air combat, a Red fighter pilot was shot down at about the same time, but he was still able to land gently with his plane in the red zone, and incidentally – by a strange coincidence – right next to the German navigator. The latter was already being heavily harassed by the Reds, some of whom in their anger were already raising their guns to liquidate him directly. Then the Russian fighter pilot swoops down on the spot, stands in front of the German and loudly rebukes the Reds: "What the hell has got into your heads?" The guys certainly grumble, but this intercession of one aviator on behalf of another makes a powerful impression on them. Slowly the gun barrels are lowered, the mob desists from the German. With a certain respect, he is led into captivity.

The Provisioning of the Sanctuary of Nuestra Señora de la Cabeza

In the course of the confrontation between the two sides, a group of Civil Guards (on the rebel side) from Jaén took refuge in the Sanctuary of Nuestra Señora la Virgen de la Cabeza on 18 July 1936, close to Andújar. Isolated since 14 September 1936, the hundred or so Civil Guards had to be supplied from the air. Spanish aviation was no novice in this type of mission, as in North Africa many garrisons had to be supplied from the air in low altitude flights. Now its objective was a surface area larger than that of a redoubt, but with the difficulty of being far behind enemy lines.

In the Sanctuary of Nuestra Señora la Virgen de la Cabeza there was not only a garrison of Civil Guards but also a civilian population, which made the arrival of supplies all the more necessary. It is estimated that the minimum daily needs of the 1,200 people under siege amounted to around 750 kilos of food and a somewhat smaller quantity of various supplies (weapons, ammunition, medicines, etc.). A communication system was set up with the besieged based on panels and codes to request food, water, medicine, ammunition, weapons and carrier pigeons and to find out the main direction of the enemy attack. Due to the resistance of the defenders, the siege lasted seven months, so it was vital to maintain communication with the besieged by air in order to achieve this.

An example of the difficult task of supplying the besieged with weapons and food took place on the 29th. Three SM.81s, three Ro.37s and nine CR.32s (flown by Italian airmen) took off from Tablada that day. Bad weather prevented the pilots from maintaining formation. In addition, some of the fighter pilots lost their orientation, going into a tailspin and crashing one of them. Another Italian pilot died during an emergency landing, three landed in enemy territory (and were captured) and another parachuted out (and was also captured).

In addition to the difficulty of delivering supplies to the besieged, the National Aviation had a second problem, which was the existence of a Republican air base in the vicinity, in Andújar. Thanks to the use of an SM.81, a certain regularity was achieved in the flights and quantities of supplies dropped to the besieged, enough to allow them to prolong their resistance (DC-2s or Ju 52s were also used). Before Christmas there was significant rationing among the besieged, which could be alleviated with nine supply drops in the last four days of 1936 and on 1 January (seven of them were carried out by Carlos de Haya in his DC-2). In the first fortnight of January 1937, not a single day was missed. The rebel side tried to give more continuity to the supply and an SM.81 was fitted out to dedicate it exclusively to this task, thanks to which in February it was possible to make 39 supply drops to the Sanctuary in 24 days of flying. But anti-aircraft fire and Republican fighters based at Andújar cut off daytime traffic in March (aggravated by the start of an attack on the Sanctuary on 26 March, which increased on 15 April) and forced night-time supply until 1 May, when the position succumbed after its leader was mortally wounded.

During the siege, it is estimated that the Sanctuary received around 100 tonnes of supplies, which were dropped in 121 missions. In addition to these missions, there were 36 bombing missions and nine reconnaissance missions (a total of 166 heavy aircraft sorties). Of these missions, 70 were flown in the SM.81, 65 with the Ju 52, another 22 with the DC-2 and nine with various other aircraft. The pilot Carlos de Haya flew more than half of these missions, becoming one of the most renowned pilots of the AN.

A brand new Nationalist Ju 52 flies over a city. This aircraft proved to be of vital importance in both transport and bombing duties.

An Italian SM.81 during a combat mission in the SCW.

The Air Battle for Málaga

After taking control of western Andalusia, the rebels tried to take control of eastern Andalusia and set Málaga as their objective. General Queipo de Llano led the attack with Spanish and Italian troops, advancing with several columns that reached the area from the south coast and from the inland mountains. The Italian ground unit CTV (*Corpo di Truppe Voplontari* or Corps of Volunteer Troops) with four divisions and air support was used as the main attacking force (a total of 39 CR.32s). Málaga was poorly defended and had little aviation: six SB-2s, some Ni52s and a few Dewoitines. These would be added to later. In defence of Málaga, six I-15s went to Torre del Mar commanded by Casimiro (the name in Spain of the Russian Anton Kovalewski) and a few Breguets, Ni52s and Vickers Vildebeest and one Potez 54 arrived in Roquetas and Tabernas.

Bombardment groups equipped with Tupolev SB-2s became tactical aviation units with excellent results as long as they had fighter protection, most notably in the rapid attack on rebel airfields.

As a curiosity, on 10 January a Heinkel He 59 of AS/88 launched a torpedo against a mail boat sailing towards Málaga, failing in its attempt. This was the first combat torpedo launch since the First World War. After that first failure, the aircraft was loaded with bombs at its base at El Atalayón (Melilla) and managed to hit the ship twice, which was left adrift due to the damage it had received.

On 14 January Estepona was occupied despite the attack of six SB-2s which failed in their attempt to stop the Nationalist advance. On the 17th, a Ni52 from Tabernas (in Almeria), two I-15 fighters and a Potez 54 bomber arrived in Marbella to support the defenders of Málaga, but it was insufficient against the four squadrons of CR.32s that had moved to the sector from the Madrid front. Queipo de Llano advanced his lines on the south coast as far as Marbella, which he occupied on the 17th. On 29 January, on the occasion of an escort service to the Sanctuary of Nuestra Señora la Virgen de la Cabeza, six CR.32s were lost due to bad weather conditions, their number being reduced from 39 to 33.

On 1 February another interesting action took place off the coast of Málaga as a patrol of three CR.32s led by Lieutenant Mantelli intercepted a pair of Potez 54s with international crews returning from bombing Motril, escorted by five I-15s commanded by Lieutenant Zakharov. The bomber escort was flying at high altitude when the three Italian aircraft appeared from the south over the sea. Mantelli fired back hitting a Potez 54, but was hit in turn by defensive gun fire which damaged the oil tank, causing the engine to overheat. As Mantelli was returning to base he was attacked by I-15s which forced him to make an emergency landing in enemy territory, although he managed to reach his own lines. The other two CR.32s managed to attack and damage the other Potez 54, causing it to make a forced landing where five of its seven crew members were injured.

On the same day, a few hours later, an Italian SM.81 and an I-15 (piloted by Casimiro) fought over Málaga. After the fighter got on the bomber's tail, he managed to shoot it down, but while it was falling, an Italian gunner managed to shoot down the Soviet pilot. The remaining five I-15s meanwhile engaged, claiming the shooting down of three enemy fighters, though no evidence has survived that this shootdown actually occurred.

On 3 February the remaining five I-15s fought against three CR.32s (two of which had to land off the field). On the 5th, two Fokkers from Tabernas returned to their base damaged, as did a He 60 seaplane of the rebels forced to ditch alongside a He 59.

Three He 59 of the Legion Condor in formation over Spanish waters.

The fighting on land continued and on 4 February Fuengirola was captured, Torremolinos on the 7th and Málaga was reached on the 8th. The support of the rebel fleet with the cruiser *Canarias* was an important aid to the attack on the city. Both the Republican Vickers Vildebeest and SB-2 had great problems with the ship's anti-aircraft artillery, failing in their attempt to sink it.

On the 11th, seven Republican planes (two Potez 54s and five I-15s) engaged CR.32s (including the three of the Blue Patrol) with one Potez 54 being shot down and another having to make a forced landing, and one CR.32, of the veteran Italian pilot Mantelli, shot down over Motril.

After the victory in Málaga, where the Spanish Squadron, already greatly reduced in men and aircraft, fought its last battles, the Nationalist command began another attack in the central part of the country. Thus, in mid-February, with this offensive concluded, the Italian CR.32s and the Blue Patrol marched towards the area near Guadalajara.

Battle of Jarama

After the victory in Málaga, the Nationalist and Italian troops were in high spirits and it was decided to cut off Madrid's communications, this time attacking from the south of the city towards the east to cut the road to Valencia and subsequently manoeuvring towards the northeast, reaching the area of Alcalá de Henares to cut the road to Barcelona. The offensive began on 6 February and was initially a success, although it ultimately failed and on 27 February the battle ended. The Nationalist side in Madrid had gone from 30 battalions in November to 75, but the Republican side had the IV and IX (commanded by Modesto), XI (Lister) XIII, XIV, XV and XVI Divisions and two groupings, plus several International Brigades for another offensive they were preparing.

On the eve of the Jarama offensive, the rebel air force was divided between the Málaga and Madrid fronts. Kindelán had 25 Spanish aircraft in Madrid (18 Ju 52s and a DH.89 at Veladas and six Ro.37s at Talavera) and 18 Italian Fiats at Torrijos reinforced by the Blue Patrol. The 30 German He 51s of the 1.J/88 hardly took part in this offensive (carrying out some escort missions). For its part, the Republican side had concentrated all the I-16s and most of the SB-2s, R-5s and R-Zs in the Central sector, while the I-15s (five squadrons) were distributed in Madrid (two squadrons), Málaga-Almeria, Aragón and the Basque Country.

On the 11th the 1st Spanish *Chatos* Squadron, commanded by García Lacalle lost its first pilot, José Calderón, shot down by the new German 88 millimetre guns, although a couple of days later it achieved its first victory. On the 12th and 13th two squadron leaders of He 51s and CR.32s were shot down, which forced the incorporation on the 14th of new CR.32s from Andalusia.

Specifically, on 12 February, He 51s piloted by *Hauptmann* Werner Palm (commander of 1.J/88) and *Unteroffizier* Hans-Jürgen were shot down by I-16 fighters. Fortunately for them, both saved their lives by parachuting over territory controlled by Nationalist troops. On 13 February the commander of the 3rd Squadron of the *Aviazione Legionaria* (Capitano Luigi Lodi) was shot down flying a CR.32bis by an I-16 jumping to land over Republican territory where he was captured. This was the fifth chief lost and the third killed so Italian morale dropped. Another notable event was the downing by mistake of a Ro.37 by He 51s of the Condor Legion.

In the case of Lodi, it is noteworthy that he flew a CR.32bis with four machine guns that in air combat represented an overweight in the aircraft (the CR.32 only carried two machine guns) that determined that the Italian command withdrew the additional armament from all CR.32bis.

These facts, which demonstrated the growing strength of the Republican fighters, led Colonel Bonami to give the order to his pilots not to enter enemy territory, as the fighters of the Legionary Aviation had been severely punished (although the CR.32s were able to compete on equal terms with the Soviet planes, the number of their own planes shot down was progressively increasing, with five pilots being shot down and killed and another five captured). The Italian fighter pilots were ordered not to cross their own lines and not to engage in combat unless at least 15 Italian aircraft were flying.

The I-16 fighter was already an experienced aircraft when it arrived in Spain, unlike the Messerschmitt Bf 109s, which were still experimental models on arrival.

Sergeant Arranz's I-15 preparing for its next mission from La Senia airfield.

The arrival in Spain of the modern Polikarpov I-16 fighters was a great relief for the FARE, which until then had relied on the I-15 biplane as its main fighter.

This is what happened on 16 February over Arganda where 11 I-15s protected by I-16s flying at a higher altitude damaged several Ju 52s, also shooting down two He 51s. This order did not sit well with some of the best Spanish pilots on the Nationalist side, who ignored the order and entered enemy territory, which led to a tense situation between Italians and Spaniards that resulted in the popularity of the so-called Blue Patrol (exclusively flown by Spanish pilots). The Blue Patrol (also known as the *Patrulla Morato*) consisted at that time of three CR.32s and three pilots as the core of the unit: Joaquín García Morato, Narciso Bermúdez de Castro and Julio Salvador.

The Italian refusal to escort the Ju 52s behind enemy lines prompted the head of the National Aviation (Alfredo Kindelán) to send the Blue Patrol to that front (which after its action in Málaga was protecting the supplies being made to the Sanctuary of Nuestra Señora la Virgen de la Cabeza). This patrol was assigned to an Italian squadron to escort the Spanish bombers with its three CR.32s.

On 18 February 1937, the Italian escort of Spanish bombers, following orders from their superiors, refused to cross the front line. But García Morato, in command of the three Spanish CR.32s (of his colleagues Salvador and Bermúdez de Castro), crossed the front line and launched into combat alone to protect the bombers (three Spanish Ju 52s and two Romeo Ro.37s) and faced more than 30 Republican fighter planes (Lacalle's I-15s supported from above by Kolesnikov's I-16s), which were already attacking the bombers. This act of great bravery encouraged the Italian pilots led by Captain Nobile who were watching the scene from afar, disobeying the orders of their superiors, to cross the front line and fight the Republican planes. The I-15s formed a 'Lufbery circle' (a defensive formation in horizontal flight devised by French fighter pilots in the First World War) as they were initially outnumbered by the Italians and Spaniards, but before long two squadrons of I-16s arrived and gave the Republicans numerical superiority.

Italian Lieutenant Degli Incerti narrated the events in this way:

> We were on our way back from an escort mission and having made sure that our bombers were safe, we had the airfield in sight and were preparing for landing. It was at that very moment that the three Spanish pilots following us decided to engage a large formation of Soviet fighters. Although the enemy aircraft were still some distance away, we made a hasty 180 degree turn at full speed and joined the fight. All the Italian fighter patrols followed us, despite the fact that we had orders to intervene only after provocation.... The fighters on both sides formed a long line of aircraft which soon began to manoeuvre sharply, and two or three "Reds" could be counted for every Nationalist aircraft. It looked as

The Fiat CR.32 3-51 belonging to the greatest Spanish ace in the SCW, Joaquín García Morato.

The mechanics are busy fine-tuning this I-15 for its next mission. The aircraft participated on all fronts with major successes.

National Aviation pilots Zorita, Pazó, Gómez Trenor, Mendía, Lacalle and Garret pose with their Fiat CR.32.

> if this formation had been planned. Tracer bullets streaked across the sky turning the duel into a hellish ballet. Trails of death smoke suddenly appeared, and the long line broke into smaller ranks. Numerous skirmishes ended inconclusively. Despite being outnumbered, we legionnaires stood together, compact, protecting each other. Suddenly, in the middle of the fight, I saw a plane catch fire and a parachute open. The first fell and crashed to the ground, while the second floated away. A "Red" had been shot down. Four of his comrades, fearing that we would shoot the pilot, surrounded the parachutist to protect him. Two CR.32s engaged them. This circumstance divided the battle into two groups, within which the fierce fighting continued. The "Curtiss" fighter section (the 1-15) broke off their attack, unable to meet our concentrated fire. They tried to escape, but this move failed and two of the retreating fighters went down in flames. Thirty minutes into the battle, thousands of bullets had streaked across the sky over Villaconejos. Then, the dance of aircraft and the rattle of machine guns ceased. The fighting slowly faded away, and before long we were left as the sole masters of the sky over the Jarama front.

García Morato's own account of this air clash is as follows:

> A few of our bombers, escorted by 21 fighters flanked by my own squadron, entered enemy territory, over which we were to hold the battle that was to decide who was to have dominion of the skies from now on. Scarcely had we reached the battlefield when 36 Red fighters began their attack on our bombers. The time had come to fight a desperate fight, all right; but then nothing seemed impossible to us. The 21 fighters of our air force seemed to hesitate. Together with the two other aircraft of my own squadron I attacked the 36 Red fighters, placing them between our bombers and them. It was a mad fight: 3 against 36. Above and below, right and left, I could see nothing but Reds. In fact, I was then convinced that this was the last battle in which I was taking part. The Chief of the 21 Nationalist aircraft, realising the difficulty of my position, and encouraged by the example of our gesture, abandoned his hesitation and ordered the whole group to go on the attack. Then things happened very quickly: one, two, three, four, five of the Red fighters crashed to the ground, one of our comrades went down in flames; three more Red fighters followed the fate of their comrades. The rest decided on a quick retreat. And our bombers, for the first time in a long time, were able to carry out the mission of bombing the enemy positions they had been tasked with. When we did the maths, we saw that eight Red aircraft had been shot down, with one loss on our part. In two more combats in the next two days, we definitively established that control of the air was ours, and we have retained it ever since.

As a result of the Blue Patrol's intervention in its first service on the Madrid front, it was awarded the Laureate Cross of San Fernando, and the other two pilots were awarded the Military Medal.

After the battle, the Republican fighters withdrew after suffering the loss of eight aircraft (four I-15s and four I-16s), four probable I-15s and one probable I-16, with only one Italian CR.32 being forced to make an emergency landing. Morato claimed a downed I-15 and would win the Laureate medal for his performance. Salvador shot down an I-16 and a second probable I-16. A remarkable fact is that, during the air battle of Jarama, with the exception of Lacalle's I-15 squadron and the Blue Patrol, the fighters were in foreign (not Spanish) hands.

On the 20th, 19 CR.32s and 28 I-15s clashed, resulting in the downing of a Polikarpov aircraft.

The Nationalist plan failed after 20 days of fighting when the offensive was stopped on the banks of the Jarama River (only managing to advance a few kilometres).

At the end of the month, 30 Heinkel He 111B bombers were handed over to the Condor Legion and began their participation in the war by bombing the airfields of Barjas and Alcalá on 9 March. They were later transferred to the north.

Despite the remarkable performance of Spanish and Italian aviation, the Nationalist side did not obtain air superiority due to the quantity and quality of the Soviet materiel and the preparation of its pilots. It was for this reason that Franco complained to the Italian ambassador and Colonel Velani (head of the *Aviazione Legionaria*) that: 'While the enemy had a large number of modern aircraft, the Nationalist side did not even have them to carry out the most necessary bombing services'. Faced with this situation, the Italian government considered two possibilities: either to abandon Spain or to reinforce its intervention, and they decided to do the latter.

On the Republican side, more aircraft continued to arrive from the Soviet Union, such as the 31 I-15s that arrived in February in Cartagena, with which a 3rd Squadron of *Chatos* was formed (which was assigned to the Aragón area) and made it possible to replace the casualties that the first two squadrons of I-15s had suffered. The three squadrons were regrouped in the so-called 26th Group, which was under the command of the Soviet Ivan Kopets (and the Northern squadron under the command of the Spaniard Felipe del Río).

Battle of Guadalajara

After the first week of March, the Italian CTV launched an offensive aimed at cutting off Madrid's communications with the west of the Peninsula by attacking from the north of Guadalajara. The result was to be disastrous for the Italians in the fighting that took place between 8 and 22 March as, although they were able to withdraw, they had to abandon much of their materiel stuck in the mud. Despite the bad weather with rain, wind and snow, the Republican air force performed adequately, but not the Italian air force, which only protected its men on the ground during the retreat (partly because its airfields were unusable due to the mud).

The FARE SB-2, R-5 and R-Z bombers supported by Lacalle's *Chatos* squadron relentlessly attacked the Italian troops and managed to stop the offensive. The greatest Republican effort was made by the SB-2s, which tirelessly attacked the enemy rearguard. The R-Zs made their SCW debut during this battle with a good performance.

On the 18th the Republican troops took the initiative and twice bombed Brihuega while I-15s strafed the troops on the ground, with Lacalle's and Kosakov's *Chatos* excelling in these actions, which completely devastated the town before the Italians could withdraw, causing panic among them. Republican planes based in Madrid strafed the marching Italian motorised columns relentlessly.

The last air combat of the battle of Guadalajara took place on 20 March when four patrols of I-15s, commanded by García Lacalle, Dahl, Tinker and García Granados, attacked three Nationalist bombers escorted by five Italian CR.32s from El Burgo de Osma. The result was one, possibly two, I-15s and one CR.32 shot down.

The battle of Guadalajara, which took place between 8 and 22 March 1937, was the last battle in central Spain, and this front became quieter while others, such as the north, increased their activity.

The Biscay Campaign, Bombardment of Guernica and the Capture of Bilbao

Given the failure of the offensives against Madrid, the rebel side ordered a new offensive in another theatre of operations that was as conducive as possible to victory. The sector chosen was the north of Spain (specifically the Cantabrian front) as there was a large area controlled by the government of the Republic that was isolated from the rest of the Republican territories. To this must be added the complicated orography and the bad weather, which made communication between the two Republican territories worse and hindered the continued use of the airfields (very close to the Cantabrian Mountains range and the sea, which made them very vulnerable). This offensive began at the end of March and ended with the victory of the Nationalists when their troops entered the Asturian towns of Gijón and Avilés at the end of October 1937 after six months of fighting.

It is estimated that in March 1937 each side could count on about 450 aircraft, more than half of which came from Italy, Germany or the Soviet Union. By this time, most of the modern aircraft that would fight in Spain were already fighting (31 I-16s, 31 SB-2s, 17 Bf 109V and B, 14 twin-engines and 12 He 70s). On 14 March the first three Bf 109As (out of a total of 14) arrived in Spain (Tablada), which would form the basis of the 2.J/88 in the following weeks.

Germany saw that the arrival of the modern Soviet aircraft required an adequate response in order to put an end to their superiority in the air. To this end, it was proposed to replace the German-piloted Ju 52s with the faster He 111s and to hand over the outdated He 51s to the Spaniards (as attack aircraft) and replace them with the modern and promising Bf 109s. J/88 consisted of Bf 109s), with 4.J/88 also consisting of He 51s. The He 51s in the Biscay raids were mainly used as ground attack aircraft, leaving the Bf 109Bs to dominate the skies and their role as fighters.

The operational debut of the R-Zs was in Guadalajara where they performed very effectively against the Italian motorised columns without suffering losses, but not as expected.

The Rasante lost its role as an assault aircraft after its poor performance in the fighting over Guadalajara and was used as a night bomber, also with little success. Another new role for the R-5s after abandoning their role as assault aircraft (where they were replaced by the Natachas) was that of coastal patrol, like the one in the photograph.

A He 70 from the *Aufsklärungstaffel* of the Condor Legion which took part in the attacks on the Catalonian power stations in January 1937.

From March 1937 the newly formed *Stuka Kette/88* unit of the Condor Legion had five Hs 123 for dive attacks. Initially they operated on the Andalusian front, but by 23 March they were already operating on the Madrid front. At the end of March (and with one Hs 123 shot down) the unit was transferred to the Vizcaya front (specifically to the Nationalist airfield at Vitoria). Also, at the end of March 2.J/88 continued its modernisation, with 24 He 51s and nine Bf 109As.

For this new offensive the air forces were deployed in bombing groups in Burgos and Soria (from where they could attack the Cantabrian Sea, the central area or Aragón) and in Vitoria the light aircraft of the Condor Legion (which was beginning to test the experimental aircraft that were arriving from Germany) which at the beginning were He 51s that were gradually replaced by modern Bf 109s. In Vitoria there were nine Messerschmitt Bf 109 fighters and in Burgos four He 111 bombers, all experimental aircraft of the squadron commanded by First Lieutenant von Moreau.

On the Republican side, initially the aircraft available in the Northern sector were few and of very different types (some I-15s and I-16s, armed Koolhoven F-51s, 30 Aero A.101s for bombing and reconnaissance and others of lesser importance). In addition, the difficulty of sending aircraft from other Republican zones or trying to do so by sea should be remembered. The *lendakari* (president of Euskadi) Aguirre made desperate requests for aircraft to the central government and except for the SB-2 bombers he was satisfied. But they were never supplied in adequate numbers and so never became a substantial air force.

The offensive began on 31 March with an attack in the Villarreal sector, in the Ochandiano area against a fortified line (20 Ju 52s protected by fighters, as well as some Heinkel He 111s and Dornier Do 17s), also a squadron of SM.81s was employed over the two main communications hubs of Durango and Elorrio (where Italian SM.81s based in Soria dropped 19 tons of bombs). He 45s and He 51s attacked in support of the troops. All Spanish, Italian

Two mechanics tune up a Bf 109 B at La Cenia airfield. The high temperature is evident from the clothing of the men.

German personnel reassembling a Heinkel He 111 E bomber of the Condor Legion in 1938. (Bundesarchiv_Bild_183-C0214-0007-013)

A Dornier Do 17 christened *Alférez Vierna* belonging to the National Aviation. This modern German-made fast bomber was known in Germany as the 'Flying Pencil'.

and German air actions were coordinated by the Condor Legion General Staff with Wolfram von Richtofen in command. Ignacio Hidalgo de Cisneros, head of the Republican air force witnessed first-hand the bombing of his airfields and the destruction of many of his aircraft during the 6th and 7th, which increased his determination not to reinforce his air force with large numbers of aircraft (and of course with modern SB-2s) at those small airfields so close to the much larger Nationalist air bases which were easy targets for their attacks.

On the 6th the Ju 52s bombed the 1st Navarre Brigade in the presence of Generals Franco and Kindelán, bombing their own troops in the capture of Sabigain. The Republican airfield at Ochandiano was captured.

Despite the initial attack, the front was stabilised between 8 and 19 April (due to the bad weather and above all to various attacks that the Republic carried out in other parts of the country such as Andalusia, Madrid and Aragón to prevent the maximum rebel effort from being concentrated in the north).

On 20 April, once the Republican attack on other fronts had been stifled in the Mondragón area, the second phase of the Nationalist offensive began, conquering Elorrio on the 24th and advancing towards Durango and Guernica. The rebel air force encountered

Three National Aviation aircraft await their next mission. In this case they are an SM.81 (21) and two Junkers Ju 52s (22).

greater opposition in the air. The reason was that the FARE had been reinforced and several pilots such as Comas, Zambudio, Zarauza, Duarte, Felipe del Río (head of the Northern *Chatos* squadron) began to fly in that sector. In one of the first bombing raids over Bilbao on 4 January, the Republican ace Felipe del Río, shot down a Ju 52 with his I-15. Three crew members were killed and the mechanical first sergeant Adolf Herman, who jumped by parachute, was captured and later savagely lynched by the mob.

In the air battles over Bilbao on 13 and 18 April, the I-15s scored three victories, including a modern German twin-engine Dornier Do 17 bomber shot down on 18 April by Felipe del Río, killing its pilot Lieutenant Hans Sobotka and forcing crew members Hoffmeister and Müller to parachute.

On 22 April, two pilots of the 2.J/88, *Leutnant* Günther Radusch and *Feldwebel* Franz Heilmayer, flying Bf 109 fighters, claimed to have shot down one I-15 each, while *Hauptmann* Lothar von Janson claimed another unconfirmed one (one of them was the one flown by Captain del Río who lost his life). In particular, the Republican ace Felipe del Río was surprised and shot down by the fast Bf 109s from Vitoria escorting his bombers as they attacked the Biscayan airfields of Sondica and Lamiaco. The Republican pilot Julián Barbero was also injured when landing at Sondica airfield due to the poor condition of the runway after the German bombing raids. After these losses, by 23 April the FARE in the north had only one I-15 in service. This squadron of I-15s deployed in the north had been given the name 'Basque Squadron' and from the arrival of the aircraft in Bilbao was commanded by Felipe Del Río Crespo. The squadron had initially been based at the Lamiaco airfield to mainly control the movements of the rebel troops in Álava.

Although the initial objective of the rebel command was the conquest of Durango, the Condor Legion command decided that the capture of Guernica was of greater importance. The Condor Legion had independent operational command and was therefore not subject to the authority of the head of the National Aviation, General Alfredo Kindelán, nor to that of the Colonel Chief of Staff, Juan Vigón, nor to that of the head of the Northern Army, Emilio Mola. This freedom, together with the discontent of the head of the Condor Legion, Sperrle, at the slow progress of the rebel troops of the Northern Army and the desire for revenge for the lynching of the crewman of a Ju 52 shot down a few days earlier over Bilbao, led to the atrocious air attack on Guernica, despite the fact that Alfredo Kindelán had forbidden the bombing of urban centres without an express order.

So, the Condor Legion sent its planes on 26 April against the Guernica sector (the intention was to besiege two retreating Basque Republican brigades occupying the Lequeitio and Marquina sectors). Reconnaissance planes mistakenly reported a concentration of troops arriving in the town, troops that in reality were apparently mixed up with locals going to the market, and the decision to bomb was justified for the Germans.

On the afternoon of that day, probably the most atrocious bombing to date took place, as 25 to 28 tons of bombs were dropped on the small town of Guernica, hitting around 25 percent of the buildings and causing a fire that spread to affect 70 percent of them. Specifically, the bombing of Guernica (where only the bridge, the road junction and the armament factories were military targets) was started by a Do 17 with 500 kilograms of bombs from Burgos at 16:30 on 26 April, heading east–west. It repeated the run, but due to the smallness of the Rentería bridge in Guernica it failed, dropping the bombs on the river, nearby houses and the church of San Juan. Before the Do 17 left, three SM 79s bombed the small bridge with 36 50kg bombs without hitting it but destroying nearby houses. Behind them came Ju 52s dropping 50 and 250kg bombs as well as 1kg incendiary bombs coated with shiny aluminium. The latter bombs were responsible for the large fire in the village. At 18:00 an experimental He 111 bombed Guernica, but with the dust and smoke it did not hit the bridge either. Between 18:30 and 19:00 19 Ju 52s (in groups of six except von Kraft's which had seven) launched another attack with most of the bombs dropped on the town. Simultaneously the four Bf 109 escorts of the 2.J/88 strafed the nearby roads full of fighters and civilians trying to escape the bombs and the voracious fire that destroyed the historic village. Curiously, the bridge at Rentería remained intact after the bombing and the Nationalist troops would later cross it in the direction of Guernica. Nationalist General Mola was deeply indignant when he learned of the destruction of Guernica.

The progressive advance of the Nationalist troops set their next target on the city of Bilbao. On 8 May the Bf 109s had shot down two SB-2s, whose speed no longer saved them from such a powerful enemy. On 22 May the so-called 'Iron Belt' (unfinished defensive positions in the vicinity of Bilbao) was reached, and on the same day one of the Hs 123s of the *Stuka Kette/88* was shot down. The attack on the Iron Belt was delayed from 31 May to 11 June by the attack on Segovia. During this period of time the Republican Northern Aviation was reinforced with two shipments of *Chatos* (15 I-15s and I-16s from Campo Soto and Algete), but an attack on the Somorrostro airfield on 5 June destroyed almost all the reinforcement planes. The Italians sent 18 CR.32s as reinforcements to the attacking troops.

In the first week of June there were various air battles in which the Italian group '*La Cucaracha*' took part, and the Bilbao airfield was also bombed. A squadron of I-15s tried to reach Bilbao from Lérida (passing through France), but on the second attempt they were forced by the French to remove their armament, after which they were allowed to fly to Santander on 31 May (although not all the planes arrived).

On 3 June, although the weather was not favourable, General Mola left Vitoria aboard the plane he usually used for his journeys, an Airspeed Envoy, which, due to the thick fog, crashed in the Brújula mountain pass, killing all the passengers.

The ruins of Guernica after bombing by Italian and German aircraft. (Bundesarchiv_Bild_183-H25224)

The great speed of the Tupolev SB-2s on their arrival in Spain made it seem as if they were invulnerable, but enemy fighters soon learned to wait for them at high altitude and then attack them in a dive.

In the attacks against the Iron Belt, on 11 May the Condor Legion lost another of its Hs 123 during a ground attack mission. On 12 June, with the support of 144 artillery pieces and 42 bombers, more than 100 tons of bombs were dropped on the Republican defensive positions. Once the Iron Belt was broken, on 18 June the Navarran Brigades entered Bilbao.

As a result of the fighting in Bilbao, with only two Hs 123 of the *Stuka Kette/88* remaining, the unit was disbanded and the two Hs 123s handed over to the AN, who used them on the Southern front.

Two CR.32s of *XVI Gruppo 'La Cucaracha'* flying in Spanish skies during one of their combat missions.

The Sinking of the Battleship *España* and other Naval Air Actions

The Spanish fleet, which included the battleships *España* and *Almirante Cervera*, was off Santander at the end of April. At dawn on the 30th, the *España*, which was to the west of Castro Urdiales, came to the aid of the destroyer *Velasco*, which was trying to stop a merchant ship. In this action, the *España* was attacked by six Gourdou Leseurre, loaded with 250kg bombs, which only slightly damaged the ship, but as it was sailing at full speed and zig-zagging, it was unable to avoid the minefield and hit one a mine, which damaged it irreparably. The *Velasco* docked alongside the *España* to rescue its crew. This situation did not go unnoticed by the head of the Republican's Northern Army who ordered his air force to finish off the *España*. The problem was that the aircraft available were not the most suitable.

Two aircraft took off from Santander and dropped some small bombs, but were repelled by the anti-aircraft armament of both ships. After the sinking of the *España*, the Republican side claimed it as a result of the action of their aircraft, although it was evidently due to the action of the mine.

During the Nationalist attack in the direction of Bilbao, an important episode of naval air combat took place during which the German battleship *Deutschland*, which was carrying out its mission in the Mediterranean Sea, hindering Republican maritime traffic in breach of international non-intervention agreements, was attacked. On 31 May, the *Deutschland* was moored off Ibiza and was bombed by SB-2s piloted by Leocadio Mendiola (despite his Basque surname, born in Badajoz) and the Soviet Leivinsky, killing 31 crew and wounding 60. It seems that this attack on a ship that was not participating in the conflict was ordered by Indalecio Prieto, Minister of Defence of the Republic, in order to put an end to the continuous German violation of neutrality.

The German retaliation was not long in coming and consisted of a bombardment of Almeria by five ships of the German fleet. In addition, Germany opted to withdraw from the Non-Intervention Committee and naval surveillance patrols until it received guarantees for its fleet.

Another military act involving the Navy and aviation took place on 14 March when the Nationalist cruiser *Almirante Cervera* captured a merchant ship from Gdynia in Poland carrying 22 Czechoslovakian Aero A.101 aircraft.

An Aero A.101 *Oca* (goose) belonging to the rebel side. This attack aircraft was used by both sides, being called *Praga* on the Republican side. Those on the rebel side were captured at sea on the ship carrying them by the cruiser *Almirante Cervera*.

The *Almirante Cervera* was also bombed and hit by the Republican air force on 22 February together with the cruisers *Canarias* and *Baleares* while bombing the port of El Grao (in Valencia) and the Sagunto blast furnaces. It was hit by several bombs which caused multiple damage and 84 casualties among its crew.

During the SCW, numerous attacks were made against warships and merchant ships, especially by the rebel side, which used its large force of seaplanes (both those of the AN and the Italians and Germans) to great effect, especially in the Mediterranean Sea sector.

Diversionary Air Operations on Secondary Fronts: Aragón (Zaragoza And Huesca)

In order to try to stop the Nationalist offensive on Vizcaya, troops from Aragón, Segovia, Madrid, Toledo and Córdoba were ordered to carry out various attacks on their fronts with the intention of forcing the Nationalist troops to reduce their actions in Vizcaya, as happened for a few days, and forcing their reserves to be scattered throughout Spain.

In Aragón, where the Nationalist side had three Heinkel squadrons (two of He 46s and one of He 51s), which were reinforced with He 46s from Asturias, commanded by Commander Vara de Rey, and the He 51 squadron from Salas. Another He 51 squadron was also sent from Seville. The combat zones were most intense in the provinces of Zaragoza and Teruel.

After the Republican troops occupied the fortified position of Santa Quitería on 12 April, eight He 46s and the available He 51s strafed the enemy trenches on the 13th, causing some 400 casualties. In this type of attack, the planes dived one after the other in single file to strafe ground targets, maintaining a continuous harassment of the ground troops, and after attacking, each plane would return behind the last one, also managing to protect each other. The most innovative aspect of this so-called *Cadenas* (chains) tactic was that it was carried out in a vertical circle for the offensive purpose of strafing enemy trenches and not horizontally, as had been done during the First World War. This tactic would later come to be used by *Luftwaffe* ground attack units in the Second World War.

The He 51s from Salas carried out the so-called chains attack, a form of attack that was proposed by García Morato and standardised three months later. The first organised chains group was actually formed in León in November 1937, initially with 12 He 51 aircraft and later with 16 (this was 1-G-2, which was officially formed on 3 December 1937 and consisted of the 1-E-2 and 2-E-2 squadrons). These He 51s from the surplus of the Condor Legion and flown by pilots from the He 45 and CR.32 were commanded by Major Muñoz Jiménez '*el Corto*'. Later the 2-G-2, 3-G-2 and 4-G-2 were formed, which were also units that carried out the chains tactic. An estimated 126 He 51s of the A-1, B-1, and C-1 versions participated during the SCW.

In Teruel there were important air clashes between the three *Chatos* squadrons (two Spanish and one Russian) and the He 51 squadrons. The one in Salas shot down an SB-2 and an I-15 on the 16th.

On the 17th there was another heavy engagement between formations on both sides. There, six Spanish He 51s (from 2-E-2) faced 10 I-15s patrolling far above them. One of the He 51s (flown by Lieutenant Palmero) inadvertently collided with an I-15, destroying both aircraft. Subsequently, 10 more Polikarpovs were added to the battle (and a little later another squadron), leaving only the five He 51s commanded by Captain Salas Larrazábal in front of them. The Nationalist pilots were clearly outnumbered, so they had to flee and managed to land at the Calamocha (Teruel) airfield with their planes completely riddled with enemy shells. The fifth He 51, piloted by Ensign Allende Isasi, was damaged in combat and forced to make an emergency landing, although it was escorted by its executioner, Sergeant Comas Borrás, who, with a chivalry typical of other times, allowed it to land in territory occupied by the Nationalist side.

García Morato, after learning of the events of the battle, congratulated Salas and recalled him to Seville, with all his pilots, to form with them the second squadron of the first all-Spanish CR.32 group, the 2-G-3. On 4 May, the two Spanish fighter squadrons became the National Aviation Group 2-G-3.

Several Heinkel He 46s during a flight. These aircraft were used for a time in the so-called *Cadenas* (chains) in coordination with the ground troops.

Diversionary Air Operations on Secondary Fronts: Segovia

Another area where at the end of May 1937 diversionary attacks were launched by the Republican army was in the area of La Granja (Segovia), in the vicinity of the Guadarrama mountain range. A good number of I-15s (two with Soviet pilots) and I-16s (two squadrons) fighter squadrons, three cooperation squadrons (two from Group 20 and one from Group 15) and the two from Group 12 of SB-2s took part, with the FARE using some 100 fighter planes. At the beginning the AN was clearly outnumbered (they had 26 CR.32s and six Ro.37s from the *Aviazione Legionaria* and six Spanish Ju 52s), but reinforcements were soon sent in (including on 1 June the ubiquitous García Morato's unit with its CR.32s, the newly formed 2-G-3) that would quickly achieve superiority in the air. Salas Larrazábal's unit and two Italian squadrons of the '*Asso di Bastoni*', one of Aero A.101s that made their combat debut, and some 10–12 He 45s were also sent, which in total would amount to some 60 planes on the Nationalist side. On the 2nd, *Zorki* (leader of the 2nd Russian *Chatos* Squadron) was shot down. He was replaced by *Kosakov*, who had already handed over the 1st to Eriomenko.

In only five days from 30 May to 4 June the Republican offensive was stopped. The number of aircraft shot down remains unknown, as the Republican side claimed seven enemy aircraft shot down and one of its own aircraft lost, while the Nationalist side claimed 10 enemy aircraft shot down. Although these figures are not confirmed, it is certain that the Nationalist side gained air dominance over the Republicans. Faced with the need for more *Katiuska* bombers for the Republic, the ship *Aldecoa* arrived in Cartagena on 24 June (with 21 SB-2-M-100-A disassembled) and several days later the *Artea Mendi* (with 10 SB-2-M-100-A). The new aircraft were assembled in San Javier and Liria, which would make it possible to create a second SB-2 Group: the 24th Group, which would be commanded by Colonel Gusaev, although it would later pass to the Spaniard Arcega. But this structure was short-lived, leaving a 12/24 Group with three squadrons (to which a fourth squadron would be added in 1938).

Diversionary Air Operations on Secondary Fronts: Aragón (Huesca)

Four days after the failure of the offensive in Segovia, a new diversionary operation was launched in Huesca in which the Republican side used a large number of aircraft. These diversionary combats lasted a week from 12 to 19 June). On the Republican side, SB-2 bombers took part, escorted by three squadrons of I-16s and two of *Chatos*, three cooperation squadrons, two of SB-2s and some Potez 54s, and on the Nationalist side, García Morato's squadron with its 13 CR.32s, already known as 2-G-3 (which moved to Zaragoza) and the Spanish squadron of He 51s (with 13 aircraft), six He 46s and six Ju 52s; totalling some 40 aircraft on the Nationalist side.

On 13 June, nine SB-2s operated over Huesca in a first raid, followed by a second raid with five SB-2s. The Zaragoza airfield was also a target for SB-2s on five occasions.

There were numerous aerial combats, as on occasions squadrons from both sides clashed, with more than 100 aircraft in combat, as occurred on the 14th of June, when the Republicans claimed 14 enemy aircraft shot down for three of their own lost aircraft, while the Nationalists claimed six downed aircraft. Specifically, on the 14th, systematic bombing of Huesca began and on the 16th all the fighter and bombing squadrons fought over the city, in a mass of around 100 planes, the Republicans having two squadrons of SB-2s, three of R-5s, two of I-15s and three of I-16s). The two SB-2 squadrons (the 1st under Proskúrov) were based at San Clemente and the 2nd under Pereira at Sisante.

Regardless of the number of aircraft shot down, the important thing was that this offensive did not yield any results for the Republican troops, as it coincided in time with the final moments of the Nationalist offensive against Bilbao, which ended with the capture of the city on 19 June. As a note of interest, García Morato's

A captured *Katiuska* is the background of this photograph taken at Tablada airfield. (Seville)

An obsolete Caudron C59 belonging to the rebel side at Zaragoza airport.

Photograph taken with a Republican *Katiuska* in the background.

CR.32 Group did not lose a single aircraft in the continuous and heavy fighting during the month of June.

Diversionary Air Operations on Secondary Fronts: Brunete

Another of the fronts opened by the Republic to try to distract Nationalist forces on the Northern Front was in Brunete (Madrid), taking advantage of the good Republican troops in the Madrid area. The fighting took place between 6 and 25 July 1937.

The first Republican attacks began on the night of 5–6 July as Republican units, under cover of darkness, penetrated deep behind enemy lines. After just over a week of heavy fighting, the Nationalist troops regained most of the ground they had initially lost, at which point the battle was over. This battle is considered one of the bloodiest of the SCW and, except for the high number of casualties on both sides, only delayed the Nationalist offensive in the North for a month longer than originally planned.

With regard to the air war, the Republican air force had numerical superiority from the outset, with four squadrons of I-16s and two of I-15s compared to three of Italian CR.32s. Most notably, the presence of García Morato's squadron was once again called for. When the Republican troops began the offensive, Morato's squadron was checking its aircraft at the Tablada (Seville) depot and had to be called up quickly. Only five planes could be sent to Ávila on 9 July 1937. The Condor Legion also sent its planes, as well as three Italian CR.32 squadrons, achieving air superiority over the Republicans. The J/88 was deployed on the Central front, the 2.J/88 in Ávila, the HQ in Valdemorillo, the 1.J/88 in Escalona del Prado and the 3.J/88 in Villa del Prado during the first half of July. Of course, the He 51s were used in attack duties and the Bf 109s as fighters. It was in July when the 17 Bf 109Bs arrived at the port of Vigo (to replace the He 51s in 1.J/88, although it already had some of the Bf 109As).

During the early morning of 7 July Ivan Yeremenko's I-15 squadron took off from Alcalá de Henares to join Lakeyev's squadron in the air. Meanwhile Minayev's squadron patrolled the front line in the Brunete area. The Republican planes came under anti-aircraft fire from their comrades defending the Delicias railway station. The Italian CR.32s arrived there and engaged in combat over the Manzanares river in the area of the Toledo Bridge. In the heat of combat, a formation of Nationalist bombers was discovered by the Republican pilots who tried to catch up with them, abandoning the fight against the CR.32s, but the Nationalist pilots pursued them and prevented any attack on their bombers. During this combat, two CR.32s were reported to have been hit in the air and destroyed. The Soviet pilots claimed to have shot down another three CR.32s during this combat. The Italians claimed the downing of seven I-15s, three I-16s and an R-Z, acknowledging the loss of only two CR.32s.

The 50th *Natachas* Squadron (R-5) that took part in these engagements was called 'Barcelona Squadron'. When the *Natachas*

Close-up of a Bf 109 C-1 of the 2.J/88th Condor Legion during 1937. This aircraft was flown by *Oberleutnant* Wolfgang Schellmann.

The R-Zs stood out in various actions such as those at Guadalajara, La Granja and Garrapinillos.

squadrons were reorganised into 30 Group, it was also known as '*El Colosal*' (The Colossal).

It was the Italian pilots who had to face the superior Republican air forces in the early stages of the battle of Brunete. For their bravery in the early stages of the battle over Brunete, they were later awarded the Collective Military Medal.

On 8 July Lieutenant Rolf Pingel, leading a *Kette* of three Bf 109s from 2.J/88 (his comrades were *Unteroffizier* Guido Höness and *Feldwebel* Peter Boddem) had an encounter with the enemy which he recounted as follows:

> As we approached the front near Madrid, *Feldwebel* Boddem observed clouds of flak around Aranjuez, I immediately turned in that direction and saw five planes flying at 3,500m towards Ávila. Blinded by the afternoon sun, I could not distinguish whether they were Nationalist aircraft, and I did not order an attack. Then I saw all the planes drop their bombs, turn around and leave in a south-easterly direction, Höness got into a favourable position for the attack. I stayed behind and watched him. After a few minutes the left engine of one of the bombers stopped turning. Then it swerved to port. Immediately after Höness's last attack I went in and fired a last burst at the bomber. The aircraft began to fall vertically with flames whirling behind both engines. No parachutes were observed. The pursuit of the other bombers had to be abandoned, as the *Kette* had penetrated 40 to 50km into enemy-controlled territory.

On that day, Condor Legion pilots Pingel and Höness claimed to have shot down the plane, which turned out to be an SB-2.

On 9 July, Republican pilot Petrovic shot down a German Bf 109, the first Bf 109 in history to be shot down. Between 10 and 11 July, air activity became more and more intense due to the arrival of new aircraft from the Nationalist side (with the Condor Legion spearheading the way with modern He 111s and Bf 109s; and the *Aviazione Legionaria* with its SM.81 and S.79). The Condor Legion units were established at the airfields of Ávila and Salamanca.

On the 12th, Morato, García Pardo and Narciso Bermúdez de Castro fought against the I-16s and 14 I-15s. During these engagements, Bermúdez de Castro's CR.32 (which was not his usual aircraft), attacked by an I-16, caught fire and crashed to the ground. In these battles west of Madrid, the Serbian pilot Petrovic with his I-15 saved his squadron commander Yeremenko from the harassment of a CR.32 (which could well have been that of García Morato) but, distracted during his movements, he did not notice the approach of another CR.32 which hit him with its projectiles and shot him down. Also, on the 12th the Bf 109B pilots of the 2.J/88 claimed the downing of two I-16s and an SB-2.

Several Bf 109 B-2s of the 2.J/88th Condor Legion during 1937. The arrival of these modern fighters began to tip the balance of the air war to the rebel side.

This photograph clearly shows one of the various camouflages used by the *Katiuskas*.

A formation of Italian S.79s belonging to the "Falchi delle Balleari" during a mission in 1937.

Between 10 and 14 July, twin-engined VB/88s acted as day bombers in the Brunete area, performing the same duties over Alcalá de Henares and Barajas on 17 and 19 July. On 23 July in the bombing of Torres de la Alameda at least seven He 111 B-1s of the VB/88 were used, with nine already in service on 1 August. The He 111 was becoming the most important bomber in the German contingent.

The fast SB-2s, known on the Nationalist side as Martins, were a tough match for the He 51s and CR.32s, but the arrival of the Bf 109s gave these Soviet-made bombers a chance of catching up. Here is *Oberleutnant* Lützow's account:

A pair of SM.81s preparing for an attack on enemy positions.

CR.32 of the Spanish ace Salas Larrazábal of the 2nd Squadron of Group 2-G-3. The fuselage reads "BERMÚDEZ PRESENTE" in memory of Captain Bermúdez de Castro who was the first Spanish CR.32 pilot killed in action on 12 July 1937.

> The battles on the Brunete front had reached their zenith, and despite our air superiority, the Red bombers attacked again and again. I was on my way back to base after a long patrol along the front over Talavera, Aranjuez, Madrid and El Escorial, when I saw clouds of anti-aircraft fire over my airfield. My eyes were literally popping out of their sockets as I struggled unsuccessfully to locate any enemy aircraft. Suddenly, off my port side and a little lower down, four "Martin" bombers appeared, heading for Madrid. I thought for a moment, should I attack or is there no point? My fuel gauge showed only a few litres left, but why let such a tasty roast escape? I turned the plane around, activated my sights and weapons and started the chase at full power. I opened fire from a great distance so that I could make use of all my ammunition in the short time I had available. The stupid thing was that the bombers were flying directly into the sun, so I only had them as faint silhouettes in front of me. To my bad luck, the bulb in my Reflex scope had blown, leaving me without any aiming device. As I figured...

One of the He 111 B-1s of VB/88 with its striking tail design. This aircraft took part in the fighting in the Brunete sector.

> I didn't hit anything! Of course I fired like a madman, uninterrupted, but before I could get close to the last of the four bombers, the barrels of my machine guns got so hot that simultaneously all three jammed. I cursed and clung to the tail of an enemy about 30m away, frantically reloading my guns. The bomber gunner seized the opportunity and fired at me, but fortunately he was so excited that he missed me. Now I had to make up my mind. Either I would break off the fight, and this was what I had to do if I wanted to reach my airfield, or I would try to unjam my machine guns and make an emergency landing due to lack of fuel. In this mountainous terrain that would be tricky…. With the heart in grief I walked away from my victim.

On the 13th, it was US pilot Frank Tinker, of the 1st 'Fly'; Squadron, who claimed to have shot down a Bf 109 in the Madrid area, flown by *Unteroffizier* Guido Höness of 2./J 88.

On the 14th the Blue Patrol (as García Morato's unit was known) managed to intercept and destroy a group of slow-moving Polikarpov R-Zs.

During the nights between 25–26th and 26–27th the Republican Night Fighter Squadron, composed of I-15s and commanded by Soviet officer Serov, achieved the first night shootdowns in history, claiming two Ju 52s. The first of these victories was over a German Ju 52 shot down between the towns of Valdemorillo and Colmenar during the night of 25–26 July by Lieutenant Mikhail Yakushin, who recounted the events as follows:

> At midnight, we received a telephone warning of a bombing raid on the Republican troops near El Escorial. It was the first time we had flown over the front after dark. The search area was outlined by fire from the bombing. Ten minutes later I saw an enemy bomber heading towards me. It didn't get away, letting it pass, I turned and began to approach at the same height from its right and from behind. By this time, we had learned that the Junkers 52's fuel tank was located near the root of the right wing. Having approached the target and slowing down, I fired at that area. Flame appeared along the right side of the bomber's fuselage at about the same time the enemy gunner responded, but it was too late. His bomber was already going down engulfed in flames. I followed it almost to the ground.

The plane was captured by Republican troops once on the ground.

By the end of July, the number of operational I-16s on the front was around 30, with at least 25 having been lost during the fighting in the Madrid area during the autumn of the previous year, and air activity was decreasing and increasing in other sectors.

Nationalist aviation ace Joaquín García Morato poses for the photographer next to the tail of his Fiat CR.32, behind him is Ángel Salas Larrazábal. Note the emblem of the yoke and arrows above the black circle on the fuselage and the Blue Patrol emblem on the tail of the aircraft.

Nice photograph of Adolf Galland's Heinkel He 51 at León airfield showing the Maltese Cross emblem on the side of the fuselage.

A curious fact during the air battles over Brunete was reported by a fighter pilot of the Condor Legion, *Oberleutnant* Günther Lützow, that when they were at their base in Ávila together with the Bf 109s they heard the sound of engines in the distance. The planes looked like SM.81s with Nationalist air force emblems that turned towards the airfield and started dropping bombs. It turned out to be a surprise attack by Potez 54 bombers with emblems similar to those of the Italian Savoia. Another curious fact about the air combat in the Brunete offensive was the combat debut of a German pilot belonging to the 3.J/88 who would become well known during the Second World War. This was Adolf Galland, who as a He 51 pilot flew ground attack missions strafing and bombing enemy troops.

After the air battles of Brunete and La Granja, the decision was taken in the FARE to relegate the Rasante to lower risk tasks due to the high number of aircraft lost in action. So the 12 R-5s that survived after the battle of Brunete were assigned to the 1st Night Flying Squadron, making their appearance in this role at the battle of Belchite.

The New Aviation Branch and The Ministry Of Defence

During the summer of 1937 there were important changes in the composition of the Republican Air Groups. There were now six air regions on the Republican side, corresponding to the combat zones: North, South, East, Centre, Extremadura and Teruel. The I-15s and I-16s were the spearhead of the FARE, as exemplified by the Republican fighters deployed in the Central sector in April 1937. Pumpur Group was formed by the squadrons: Lacalle (27 I-15s at Guadalajara), Zotsenko (13 I-15s at Andújar), Osadchii (15 I-15s at Castellón) and Kolesnikov (24 I-16s at Tembleque), of which 62 were in service and 17 under repair. The air groups deployed in Valencia in June 1937, according to Salas Larrazábal, consisted of: Group 12 (24 SB-2s in two squadrons), Group 15 (25 R-5s in three squadrons), Group 20 (24 R-Zs in two squadrons), Group 21 (with 60 I-16s in five squadrons), Group 25 (with 30 R-Zs in three squadrons), Group 26 (with 48 I-15s in three squadrons) and Group 30 (30 R-Zs in three squadrons), making a total of 241 aircraft.

During the battles of Jarama, Guadalajara, La Granja, Huesca, Brunete and the Northern sector, a large number of I-16s had been lost, which were replaced with the arrival of the ship *Cabo de San Agustín*, which carried 62 Type 6 I-16s. This shipment brought the total number of I-16s arriving in Spain to 155. Some of them were sent to the High Speed School based in El Carmolí (Murcia).

Prior to this, on 1 May 1937, a new batch of 31 SB-2s arrived, with which Group 24 (with three squadrons) was created. Characteristically, this Group was made up mainly of Soviets, unlike the 12th Group, also of SB-2s, which was dominated by Spaniards. The summer of 1937 also saw the replacement of Groups 20 and 25 by three independent squadrons.

One of the novelties was the creation of an experimental night fighter squadron, commanded by Anatoli Serov, with I-15s and exclusively Soviet pilots, although by 1938 it would be composed only of Spanish pilots.

Another change in the FARE from the summer of 1937 was the order that R-Zs should always operate under escort as a result of the increasing number of Nationalist fighters. In addition, the 20th and 25th R-Z Groups were disbanded into three Independent Squadrons (the 20th, 40th and 50th Squadrons). These three squadrons were reinforced (due to casualties suffered) and a 4th Squadron (named 4th Squadron of 30 Group) was created in September 1937. There were 15 aircraft per squadron (12 combat ready and three in reserve). Table 8 shows the deployment of the FARE according to Salas Larrazábal.

Table 8: Deployment of the FARE between September 1937 and April 1938

Squadron No. 11	
Group 21	1st, 2nd, 3rd, 3rd, 4th, 5th and 6th Squadrons
Group 26	1st, 2nd, 3rd and 4th Squadrons
Night Flight Squadron	
Squadron No. 5	
Group 24	1st, 2nd, 3rd and 4th Squadrons
Group 30	1st, 2nd, 3rd and 4th Squadrons
Squadron No. 7	
Group 71	1st, 2nd, 3rd and 4th Squadrons
Group 72	1st, 2nd, 3rd and 4th Squadrons
No. 6 Seaplane Group	1st, 2nd and 3rd Squadrons
1st Night Flight Squadron	

Also in the National Aviation, the increasing arrival of new aircraft from its German and Italian allies led to the restructuring of the entire air force. It is true that the changes were not abrupt and punctual but progressive, so that the distribution shown in Table

Seven squadrons of I-16 fighters were formed in the FARE belonging to Group 21.

Initially the R-Zs were assigned to Group 20, made up of two squadrons (20 and 50) which in September 1937 would form Group 30.

Poor quality but very interesting photograph of a *Chato* of the 1st Night Fighter Squadron.

9 would correspond to the basic structure of the AN between May 1937 and April 1938 (although later there were still changes and new units to be added to the AN).

Table 9: Basic structure of the AN between May 1937 and April 1938

UNIT	COMPOSITION
1-G-2	1-E-2
	2-E-2
2-G-3	1-E-3
	2-E-3
3-G-3	3-E-3
	4-E-3
1-G-10	1-E-10
	2-E-10
2-G-10	3-E-10
	4-E-10
3-G-11	1-E-11
	2-E-11
4-G-12	1-E-12
	2-E-12
5-G-17	1-E-17
	2-E-17
6-G-15	1-E-15
	2-E-15
1-G-2 means 1st Group of Type 2 aircraft (in this case the Heinkel He 51 shown in the annexes). 1-E-2 refers to the 1st Squadron of Type 2 aircraft.	

1-G-3 was created in April 1937 after the acquisition of more CR.32s from Italy, with which the 1st Squadron (1-E-3) was formed and at the end of April the 2nd Squadron (2-E-3) was formed.

Table 10: Squadrons created within the National Aviation

Unit	**Composition**
Squadron No. 1	
1-G-22	1-E-22
	2-E-22
2-G-22	3-E-22
	4-E-22
Squadron No. 2	
3-G-28	1-E-28
	2-E-28
4-G-28	3-E-28
	4-E-28
Squadron No. 3	
5-G-28	5-E-28
	6-E-28
7-G-14	1-E-14
	2-E-14
	3-E-14
	4-E-14
Additional units	
1-G-70	1-E-70
	2-E-70
2-G-62	1-E-62
	2-E-62
1-E-60	

Note that the Spanish Groups had two squadrons, although in 1938 the two Groups of fighters with CR.32s (2-G-3 and 3-G-3) came to form a third squadron; reaching four squadrons in 2-G-3 at the end of the SCW.

In the case of the Condor Legion and *Aviazione Legionaria* fighter groups, they had 36 aircraft on their payroll, although they rarely reached these figures. The Condor Legion squadrons usually had 12 aircraft, as did the Italian squadrons, although between March and October 1937 they were reduced to 10. The National Aviation squadrons started with only six or seven aircraft, rising to nine per squadron by the end of 1937.

Table 11: Deployment of the *Aviazione Legionaria*, August 1937

Fighter Squadrons under *3rd Stormo Caccia dell'Aviazione Legionaria*	
XVI Gruppo *'La Cucaracha'* (The Cockroach Group) *Maggiore* (Major) Giuseppe Casero	26th (subsequently renamed 2nd) Squadron
	24th (4th) Squadron
	25th (5th) Squadron
XXIII Gruppo 'Asso di Bastoni' (Asso di Bastoni Group) *Maggiore* Andrea Zotti	18th (2nd) Squadron 19th (1st) Squadron 20th (6th) Squadron
VI 'Gamba di Ferro' Gruppo *Maggiore* Eugenio Lotta	31st (7th) Squadron 32nd (8th) Squadron 33rd Squadron (from 1 October)
Bombardment Squadron	
XXIV Gruppo Pesado (Heavy Group)	213th Squadron
	214th Squadron
	215th Squadron
XXIX Gruppo Veloz (Fast Group)	280th Squadron 289th Squadron Patrol Br.20
Other units	
XXXV Gruppo Autónomo (Autonomous Group)	Br.20 Squadron
	Ba.65 Squadron
XXII Gruppo de Reconocimiento (Reconnaissance Group)	120th Squadron 128th Squadron
Aviazione Legionaria delle Baleari	
XLI Gruppo de Bombardeo Veloz (Lightning Bombardment Group)	1st Squadron (101st later) 2nd Squadron (102nd)
X Gruppo Autonomo de Caccia (Autonomous Fighter Group)	1st Squadron 2nd Squadron
Patrulla Macchi Patrol M.41 (Macchi Patrol M.41)	
Escuadrilla Savoia Savoia SM.81 (Squadron SM.81)	

At the beginning of April 1937, the rebel forces had: 14 Bf 109s, 85 CR.32s, 71 Ro.41s, 62 SM.81s and Ju 52s, 17 He 45s and He 70s, 42 Br. XIXs and He 46s, among other aircraft deployed in the various sectors of the front. Although the number of aircraft varied continuously due to the fighting and the arrival of new aircraft.

A National Aviation SM.81 belonging to 16-G-21 waits at an airfield for its next mission.

Italian fighter pilots enlisted in La Legion to fly the CR.32 also supplied by Italy.

Several SM.81s during a bombing raid on Republican positions.

The Do 17 F-1s arrived in Spain to replace the He 70 *Rayo* on reconnaissance missions in March 1937.

The Nationalist side ordered 26 S.79s from Italy, the first of these aircraft being delivered in August 1937. With the arrival of the S.79s, the 3-G-28 Group (with eight S.79s), the 4-G-28 (at the end of 1937), the 5-G-28 and the 6-G-28 (in the spring of 1938) were organised.

For its part, the Condor Legion maintained the structure shown in Table 12 after the arrival of the new material from Germany in March 1937.

Table 12: Condor Legion organisation, March 1937

Jagdgruppe J/88 (Major Hubertus Merhardt von Bernegg)	*Jagdgruppe J/88* (commanded by Major Hubertus Merhardt von Bernegg)
	Jagdstaffel 1.J/88 Marabu (12 Messerschmitt Bf 109 B1)
	Jagdstaffel 2.J/88 Zylinderhut ("Top Hat") (12 Messerschmitt Bf 109 B1)
	Jagdstaffel 3.J/88 Mickymaus ("Mickey Mouse") (12 Heinkel He 51)
	Versuchsjagdstaffel VJ/88 (experimental squadron with Messerschmitt Bf 109, Henschel Hs 123, Heinkel He 112V and Junkers Ju-87A-0)
Kampfgruppe K/88 (Major Robert Fuchs)	Kampfstaffel 1.K/88 (12 Junkers Ju 52)
	Kampfstaffel 2.K/88 (12 Junkers Ju 52)
	Kampfstaffel 3.K/88 (12 Junkers Ju 52)
	Versuchsbomberstaffel VB/88 (experimental squadron with Heinkel He 111, Dornier Do 17 and Junkers Ju 86), commanded by *Oberleutnant* von Moreau
Aufklärungsstaffel A/88	
Gemischte Aufklärungs- und Bombenstaffel See AS/88	

The German unit underwent a further reorganisation in October 1937, including the replacement of its General Hugo Sperrle by Helmuth Volkmann and its Chief of Staff, Wolfram von Richthofen, by Hermann Plocher, and with the arrival of new aircraft its organisation became as shown in Table 13.

Table 13: Condor Legion organisation, October 1937

Führungsstab S/88, command and staff (commanded by General Helmuth Volkmann and Colonel Hermann Plocher). With liaison aircraft Fi 156 A, Messerschmitt Bf 108 and Junkers W 34.	
Jagdgruppe J/88 (Major Gotthard Handrick)	*Jagdstaffel 1.J/88 Marabu* (12 Messerschmitt Bf 109)
	Jagdstaffel 2.J/88 Zylinderhut ("Top Hat") (12 Messerschmitt Bf 109)
	Jagdstaffel 3.J/88 Mickymaus ("Mickey Mouse") (12 Messerschmitt Bf 109)
	Jagdstaffel 4.J/88 (12 Heinkel He 51)
Kampfgruppe K/88 (Major Carl von Wechmar)	*Kampfstaffel 1.K/88* (12 Heinkel He 111)
	Kampfstaffel 2.K/88 (12 Heinkel He 111)
	Kampfstaffel 3.K/88 (12 Heinkel He 111)
	Kampfstaffel 4.K/88 (some Ju 52 mainly for night operations)
Aufklärungsstaffel A/88 (12 Dornier Do-17 and 6 Heinkel He 45)	
Gemischte Aufklärungs- und Bombenstaffel See AS/88 (He-59 and He-60 based in Pollensa)	
Luftnachrichten-Abteilung (mot.) Ln/88 (with four *Kompanies*)	
Flak Abteilung F/88, Motorised Anti-Aircraft Group with five 88mm heavy batteries (*Schwere*), two 20mm light batteries (*Leichte*) supported by a 37mm section and a group of searchlights and rangefinders.	

It is important to note that the 88mm guns were modern artillery pieces that could reach air or ground targets at long ranges and with a high volume of fire. They would also prove their great effectiveness during the Second World War.

A Dornier Do 17 damaged by enemy anti-aircraft artillery and forced to make an emergency landing.

One of the fast Do 17s that were used in reconnaissance and fast bombing duties during the SCW.

A mechanic is tuning a Bf 109 of the 2.J/88 *Zylinderhut* for its next mission.

The He 112V3 after a crash landing on 19 July 1937. The aircraft was taken out of service.

Rear of the Bf 109 D-1 of 3.J/88 flown by ace Werner Mölders. This aircraft called *Luchs* shows at that time 12 victory bars on the rudder.

Several He 111 Bs wait at a Nationalist airfield. During the SCW, the He 111 gradually became the most important bomber in the German arsenal.

A He 70 F with green camouflage belonging to the Stab/K88 in 1937, showing a small pigeon emblem under the cockpit.

A Do 17E from the Condor Legion A/88 awaiting its next mission.

A Dornier Do 17 P-1 (with its distinctive distinctive radial engines) reconnaissance aircraft arrived in December 1937 to join the A/88.

The Battle of Santander

Once the city of Bilbao had been captured, the Nationalist troops began the task of completely wiping out the territory held by the Republic in the north of the country. The offensive to the west was therefore prepared, with Santander as the first objective, followed by the conquest of Asturias. In this way, the Republic would lose a large part of its territory and, above all, the possibility of the arrival of military materiel via the Cantabrian Sea (once the Republic had been deprived of Basque industries and communication with France via the Basque Country). An example of the arrival of military materiel by sea, despite the naval blockade by the rebels, with the *Almirante Cervera* as the most powerful ship, was the arrival at the port of Musel (Gijón) on 3 July of the Estonian merchant ship *Viiu* carrying eight Bristol Bulldogs and six Potez 25A.2 disassembled.

The number of ground troops on both sides was slightly higher among the defenders. In the air, the Republic had two fighter squadrons (I-16s and I-15s) and another two cooperation squadrons (with Bristol Bulldog and other varied aircraft); while on the Nationalist side, five squadrons of modern, fast aircraft were deployed in the area (Bf 109B fighters, He 111 twin-engine bombers, a mixed squadron of Do 17 and He 70 and the Italian squadrons of S.79 and Ba.65); seven of CR.32 biplane fighters (five Italian and two from García Morato's group), as well as several less modern aircraft (Ju 52, He 45 and Aero A.101). Once the offensive had begun, the Republic managed to send a new squadron of I-16s to Santander, commanded by Smirnov but with a majority of Spanish pilots, and some I-15s. Despite the Republican reinforcements, the air battle was expected to be completely dominated by the rebels, although the FARE showed a lot of resistance.

The offensive against Santander began on 14 August, the day on which the He 45s and Aero A.101s, protected by Nationalist aircraft including García Morato's CR.32s, acted without encountering practically any enemy air opposition. The Condor Legion, for its part, shot down several enemy aircraft during this offensive.

According to the rebel side, between 21st and 23rd the FARE lost some 30 aircraft of various types to the Italian '*Gamba di Ferro*' group alone, although these figures are unconfirmed. On the ground the advance was relatively easy for the rebels (the city fell on 22 August) while in the air they also managed to dominate, but with greater difficulties. The FARE based in the 6th Air Region lost 17 I-15s, 10 I-16s and some 30 aircraft of various types; while the Nationalist side lost seven aircraft at the front (one Ju 52, one Do 17, one He

Several Dornier Do 17s waiting for their next mission at their airfield.

A Bf 109 B in the foreground with several others in the background. This aircraft replaced the He 51 in the fighter role in the Condor Legion.

An Aero A.101 *Oca* from the Nationalist side, fresh from an overhaul at Tablada aerodrome (Seville).

The pilot poses proudly on his I-15 belonging to the 3rd Squadron of *Chatos* at La Rabasa.

111, two He 51s and two Ro.37s) and four in landing accidents (one CR.32, one Bf 109, one He 111 and one He 45). Between 14 and 26 August the Bf 109s of 2.J/88 (with Bf 109B) managed to shoot down 11 enemy aircraft without losing a single aircraft.

The Battle of Belchite

Between 24 August and 6 September 1937, this battle was fought by the offensive of the Popular Army (Republicans) in the direction of Zaragoza (attacking from the south, east and north of the city) with some 80,000 men and a hundred tanks. The first fighting around Belchite began between 24 and 25 August and the air force on both sides played an important role. In this case the FARE had numerical superiority over the National Aviation. In terms of fighters, the FARE had two Russian squadrons of I-16s, another squadron (with several Spanish pilots), two squadrons of I-15s piloted by Russians and another squadron of I-15s piloted by Spaniards. To this must be added six squadrons of R-Zs and three of SB-2s (two of them piloted by Spaniards). For their part, the Nationalists only had the He 46 group, one Ju 52 squadron and one (Spanish) He 51 squadron in the area. Once the offensive began, the Italian CR.32 '*Asso di Bastoni*' Group and the CR.32 Group of García Morato (2-G-3) were sent urgently to the sector from Madrid and Santander respectively. Subsequently, the 31st and 32nd *Squadriglie* of the VI Gruppo were sent by the Italians.

The Republican superiority in the air also caused significant losses on the Nationalist side, as Captain Enrico degli Incerti recounts:

> During an escort mission flown through clouds, we perceived the presence of a formation of I-15 fighters flying below us as we crossed some clearings. I dropped down, followed by my patrol, and as I emerged from some clouds, I found myself in an excellent position behind one of the I-15s. Five short bursts and the enemy fighter began to drop. I followed it until I saw it crash into the Ebro River. As I tried to gain altitude, I spotted

One of the fast SB-2s used by the FARE and which the Nationalist side had to learn to fight because of their high speed.

> five enemy fighters heading straight for me. The patrol leader attacked me while the rest flew around me firing bursts at close range. The bullets shattered the windscreen, damaged the parachute and punctured the fuselage. I dived to try to shake off my pursuers, but to no avail… At one point I found myself on the tail of the I-15 patrol leader, tried to shoot him down, but was instantly hit by a burst, wounding my leg. I tried to escape by accelerating, but my Fiat was not responding well and I felt a thin line of black smoke start to emit. I descended as fast as I could, with a hail of bullets whistling around me and hitting the plane, which, miraculously, was still flying. Chased by the I-15s I was already approaching the ground, smelling the smoke and sensing the rapidly rising heat of the burning fuselage. The engine stopped suddenly when I was only a few metres from the ground. I turned off the fuel and dropped the plane. The tail of the burning Fiat rose into the air and fell back to the ground.

An Italian-made Fiat Br.20 bomber during bomb loading. These aircraft arrived in Spain in July 1937 (specifically in Seville) and were integrated into the 230th Bombing Squadron of the Aviazione Legionaria. Later this squadron together with the 231st and 65th Squadrons were added to the 23rd Group of the National Aviation.

During the 26th, one He 46, flown by the commander of the He 46 group, Major Pérez Pardo, and one He 51 from the Nationalist side were shot down.

In this battle the Republican R-5s of the 1st Night Flying Squadron, based in Caspe, performed for the first time. The mode of attack was 'one at a time' bombing, suffering no casualties in the face of enemy fire. Both the R-5s and R-Zs suffered heavy casualties in the battle (the R-Zs lost 18 aircraft between Brunete and Belchite).

After the first days of the Republican offensive, the Nationalist forces in Zaragoza began to react on 31 August. At this time the newly created Spanish group of Savoia S.79s (3-G-28), another group of Ju 52s and the other (Spanish) squadron of He 51s that also came from Santander, including Bf 109B fighters from La Albericia (Santander), joined the fight. The German participation was not very important, although they did send their He 111 and Bf 109B squadrons for a short period of time.

In one of the dogfights near Belchite, during a Ju 52 raid, some of their Italian escort fighters broke off to attack 11 SB-2s, of which the Italian CR.32 pilots claimed 10 shot down.

The Condor Legion played an effective role in bombing the Republican artillery batteries, while the Italian *Aviazione Legionaria* also participated in the bombing raids, with the new Br.20 bombers and the ubiquitous CR.32s. Italian CR.32s and German He 51s were the escorts for the transport planes and bombers on the missions around Belchite.

Three Spanish Ju 52s dropped ammunition, food, medicine, sacks and mail on a daily basis. One of them was piloted by the famous pilot Carlos de Haya, who flew his Ju 52 and made multiple low flights over the Nationalist troops besieged in the town, under intense anti-aircraft fire and the omnipresent Republican fighters. During these dangerous flights they managed to supply the defenders of Belchite with medicines, food and ammunition, which proved to be of great importance in the defence of the town.

The Nationalist counteroffensive took place on 30 August using 10 Ju 52s, supported by 21 fighters, which helped defeat the Republican attackers at Belchite.

On 1 September García Morato's group was mainly engaged in this battle in support of the ground forces together with the He 51. On the same day, one He 51 and one He 46 were shot down. García Morato's group 'took revenge' the next day during an engagement with I-15s, of which they shot down two. García Morato's Spanish

Group 2-G-3 claimed overall the downing of seven I-15s over Belchite, according to Logoluso this was five I-15s and two I-16s).

On the night between 14–15 September a Ju 52 was shot down during a night bombing mission over Sariñena airfield.

Battle for Asturias

After the capture of Santander, the Republican forces in the north were reduced to the province of Asturias and it was only a matter of time before they were defeated. The Asturias Campaign began in September with little resistance from the Republican forces and ended the following month with the entry of the Navarran Brigades into Gijón and Avilés.

The FARE in Asturias was mainly represented by the Northern Aviation fighter squadron where a handful of I-15s and I-16s were completely outnumbered by their enemies. The superior National Aviation had five squadrons of modern Condor Legion aircraft (two of Bf 109Bs, two He 111s and one reconnaissance). For their part, the Spanish planes on the Nationalist side were used to support the ground troops and for ground attack (several planes were shot down by anti-aircraft artillery); specifically, on 9 September, García Morato's group supported the attack by A.101s and He 45s that were attacking enemy positions.

Sergeant Miguel Zambudio (who was to become an outstanding pilot in the FARE), was shot down by a Bf 109B over the town of Llanes, although he managed to land wounded and with his biplane on fire, abandon the aircraft and reach his lines. Once Llanes was captured, the unit of which Adolf Galland was a member was deployed at his airfield, of which he commented: 'Llanes was the most curious airfield from which I have ever taken off. Situated on a plateau in front of a cliff, with the remaining three sides almost as steep, it was like taking off from the roof of a skyscraper on the seashore'.

Impressive photograph of a Heinkel He 45 during a mission. These aircraft were mainly used as reconnaissance aircraft.

The German pilot, *Leutnant* Eduard Neumann, achieved his first victory over Asturias as he recounted: 'During my first operational flight over Asturias on 4 September 1937, I was flying behind Galland when I saw a Polikarpov I-15… and I shot it down. It was very difficult to do that with a He 51.'

On 4 September the Nationalists entered Asturias, on the 11th they occupied Cangas de Onís, and later in their triumphal advance they captured the port of Musel where the planes of the Condor Legion sank the destroyer *Ciscar* and the submarine C.6. It was on the 21st in Gijón where they captured a squadron of I-15s (four planes) and another of 1-16s (four planes, one of which was transported by ship from Vigo to Germany to be studied). In fact, the FARE lost four fighters in combat, but most of its aircraft in Asturias were destroyed on the ground. The Condor Legion during these engagements lost one Do 17 (that of the reconnaissance squadron leader) and three of the He 111s had to make forced landings due to damage from Republican fighters.

In late September several air engagements took place over Gijón where German Bf 109Bs engaged enemy I-15s and I-16s. In one of these engagements five Bf 109Bs from 1.J/88 clashed with five I-16s, with *Oberleutnant* Harro Harder claiming to shoot down one enemy fighter as well as forcing another to land, while *Leutnant* Erich Woitke claimed another I-16. The Germans suffered no casualties in this engagement. Just one day later another Bf 109B shot down an I-16 flown by the commander of the Northern '*Mosca*' squadron, Lieutenant Andrés Rodríguez Panadero.

With the fall of Asturias, the Northern campaign ended, causing a major strategic shift in the SCW. The Republic had lost at least 60 I-15s in the Cantabrian area (to which must be added those lost in other areas of Spain) and a smaller number of I-16s. These losses were very significant for the Republic, which always needed more and more aircraft.

On the other hand, the Nationalist side eliminated the constant danger of an enemy to the north and was able to send land and air units that were deployed in the Cantabrian Sea to other sectors. The war continued and every day the Republican side would find it more difficult to win a victory, a victory that would never come. Moreover, the warships that were deployed in the Bay of Biscay could be sent to the Mediterranean (where the island of Majorca became the main

A He 111 displaying the typical insignia of the rebel side.

Nationalist base of operations) and block the way for war materiel to reach the Republic via the Mediterranean. The Soviet Union had to use other routes (North Atlantic and Baltic routes to the French Atlantic ports) that were much more complicated, which meant that the supplies that the Republic received were greatly reduced. Meanwhile, the Nationalist side continued to receive large quantities of military equipment from allied Germany and Italy. These changes also had consequences for the air war, which became increasingly advantageous for the Nationalist side.

An important event in the Condor Legion was the replacement of Hugo Sperrle on 1 November 1937 by Hellmuth Volkmann, who remained in that position until 31 October 1938.

Between October and December 1937, 90 modern aircraft arrived in Spain from Italy and Germany, plus 154 older type aircraft (86 CR.32s, 36 He 51s and 22 of other types). With these acquisitions, the AN would have some 400 combat aircraft.

This allowed the creation of two new Spanish S.79 Groups and the 1st Spanish Air Brigade, under the command of Colonel Sáenz de Buruaga. The 1st Air Brigade was composed of three Squadrons (the 1st commanded by Eduardo González Gallarza with Ju 52s, the 2nd commanded by Lacalle Larraga with S.79s and He 70s and the 3rd commanded by Orleans with S.79s and He 70s). To complement the 1st Air Brigade, the 2-G-3 and 3-G-3 Fighter Groups were joined, the latter being created at the beginning of December 1937.

On the Republican side, during the same period of October to December 1937, the Republican air force only incorporated 10 SB-2 twin-engines and 35 I-15s of Spanish manufacture, delivered by the Reus-Sabadel factory.

After the end of the fighting on the Northern front, García Morato's group increased the number of aircraft in its squadrons to nine (as mentioned earlier in December, when the 3rd and 4th Spanish Fiat CR.32 squadrons were formed, the 3-G-3 was created with them). Another important event for the AN was the creation of the 1st Hispanic Air Brigade after the Northern campaign, which included some 150 aircraft of various types, always manned by Spaniards.

Continuation of the Battle Of Belchite

When the end was in sight for the Republican army in Asturias, the Republican army in the East restarted the offensive with the aim of reaching Zaragoza. Once again, the air forces of both sides had to engage in bloody clashes in which the Republican pilots achieved important successes.

On 12 October the I-16s shot down five Italian CR.32s of the '*Asso di Bastoni*' Group (one of them that of a squadron commander), losing two I-15s and two I-16s (from the 21st and 26th Groups). Three days later the 1st and 2nd '*Chatos*' squadrons with 21 I-15s (commanded by Antonov and Gerardo Gil) commanded by the 26th Group commander (the Spaniard Juan José Armario) and R-5s attacked at dawn and by surprise the Nationalist airfield at Sanjurjo/Garrapinillos (Zaragoza) while 34 I-16s protected them from the heights. The result was the destruction on the ground of eight CR.32s and damage to at least three Ju 52/3mg, which, being loaded with bombs, exploded damaging six He 46s. In this attack the protection of the I-15 aircraft was provided by the 1st, 2nd, 5th and 6th '*Mosca*' squadrons, commanded by Aguirre, Pleschenko, Smirnov, Ivanov and Gusiev).

The battle of Belchite finally ended because the Republic had failed to achieve its objectives of containing the Nationalist advance from the north and conquering a large part of the territory controlled by the Nationalists.

One of the *Mosca* belonging to the 4th Squadron of the 21st Group as can be seen by the "Popeye" painted on its tail.

The Tupolev SB-2Ms sent to Spain were the most modern bomber aircraft available to the Soviet Union.

A Heinkel He 46 from the Nationalist side known as the "Pava" (turkey hen) because of its slow flight. The first 12 aircraft of this model arrived in Seville in September 1936 and were incorporated into Group 11.

Nice picture of a Gonzalez Pazó GP-1 training aircraft belonging to the Republicans.

One of the 15 or so Nieuport 52C.1s that remained in the hands of the rebels at the beginning of the SCW. This one still carries the Republican colours.

A Gil-Pazó GP-2 light aircraft belonging to the rebel forces.

A Fiat CR.32 that was captured by the Republican side is seen during one of its trials with its new owners, in this case at El Carmolí or San Javier.

Two Arado Ar 68s on the runway, waiting for their next mission.

The modern Italian-built Cant Z.506 seaplane on the ground platform at its base in Pollensa shows its newly painted insignia.

A photograph of a Caudron C59 with Nationalist insignia.

A Gil-Pazó liaison aircraft belonging to the Hispanic brigade. Behind it is a Savoia SM.81 bomber.

The pressing need for aircraft on both sides meant that many of them were purchased in very small numbers. The aircraft numbered 31 were twin-engine aircraft of various origins.

As with the image to the left, the number 30 was used for single-engine aircraft of various origins and models.

Nice photograph of a Cant Z.506 of the National Aviation during combat service.

BIBLIOGRAPHY

Principal Sources

Abellán, Juan. *Galería de aviones de la Guerra Civil Española (1936-1939)* (Ministerio de Defensa, 2003)
Arias Ramos, Raúl. *Legión Cóndor* (Almena, 2000)
Arráez Cerdá, Juan. *Archivos fotográficos y documentales.*
Fresno, Carlos; Montera, Artemio. *Aviones de la Guerra Civil Española* (Abteilung 502, 2021)
Gil Martínez, Eduardo Manuel. *La fuerza aérea española durante la 2ª guerra mundial* (Almena, 2019)
Martínez Canales, Francisco. *Cazas y Ases en España. 1936/39* (Almena, 2020)
Pecker, Beatriz; Pérez, Carlos. *Crónica de la Aviación Española* (Sílex, 1983)
Salas Larrazábal, J. *La Guerra Civil 1939-39* (Aeroplano. Nº 29, 2011)
Salas Larrazábal, J. *La caza republicana en la Guerra Civil Española* (Ministerio de Defensa, 2000)

Secondary Bibliography/Additional Reading

Evans, Steve A.; Jekl, Libor, *The Spanish Civil War. Prelude to World War II* (Valiant Wings, 2016)
Forsyth, Robert, *Aces of the Legion Condor* (Osprey, 2011)
Forsyth, Robert, *Ju 52/3m Bomber and Transport units 1936-41* (Osprey, 2017)
Galán Ortega, José, *Representación de la lucha en el aire* (Revista Universitaria de Historia Militar, Volumen 7, 2018)
García, Dionisio, *FIAT CR-32 "Chirri"* (Ikonos Press, 2022)
García Morato, Joaquín, *Guerra en el aire* (Galland Books, 2008)
Gori, Cesare, *S.79* (La Bancarella Aeronautica, 2008)
Logoluso, Alfredo, *Fiat CR.32 Aces of the Spanish Civil War* (Osprey, 2010)
Permuy, Rafael A, *Spanish Republican Aces* (Osprey, 2012)
Permuy, Rafael A.; Molina, Lucas, *Unidades experimentales de la Legión Cóndor* (Galland Books, 2013)
Permuy, Rafael A., *Atlas ilustrado de la Aviación en la Guerra Civil Española* (Susaeta, 2014)
Pototsky, Oleg, *I-16. Rata* (Kagero, 2021)
Salas, Jesús; de Madariaga, Rafael, *Túpoliev SB Katiuska en España (Vol. I) Histórica 36/39* (Quirón Ediciones, 2000)
Tarazona, Francisco, *Yo fui piloto de caza* (San Martín, 1974)
Trautloft, Hannes, *Piloto de caza en la guerra de España* (Galland Books, 2020)

Online Resources

La aviación de la República. (1936-1939) – A.D.A.R. (adar.es)
Historia de las Fuerzas Aéreas de la República Española - Wikipedia, la enciclopedia libre
Modelismo militar e Historia: El Polikarpov I-16 en España
LAS ESCUADRILLAS Y EMBLEMAS DE LA «GLORIOSA» : AVIACIÓN REPUBLICANA – A.D.A.R. (adar.es)
es.wikipedia.org
Memoria Republicana - Imágenes FARE (sbhac.net)

ABOUT THE AUTHORS

Eduardo Manuel Gil Martínez has been an enthusiast of Spanish military history for many years, mainly focussing on the Second World War and the Reconquista (Middle Age in Spain). He has been the author of many history articles in Spanish and Italian magazines and more than 40 books about the Second World War in several languages (Spanish, English, Italian and French) for several top publishers. His previous works for Helion include *The Blue Squadrons. The Spanish in the Luftwaffe. 1941-1944* and *Fallschirmjäger in the Defence of the Oder. 1945.*

The late Juan Arráez Cerdá was a Spanish aviation expert and owner of one of the best picture collections of Spanish aviation. He authored many books and articles about aviation in French and Spanish and co-authored *The Blue Squadrons. The Spanish in the Luftwaffe, 1941–1944* for Helion and Company.